Mrs Mooney 100 years old on

Monday.

8 August.

Card from Mayor

Mrs Mooney.
3 Gould Close
North dimms.

Hat Herts.

17 Aug for one week on holiday.

WONDERFUL WINDOWBOXES

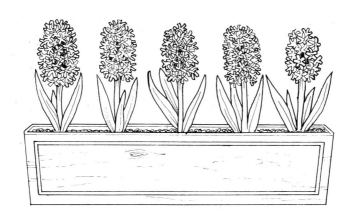

WONDERFUL
WINDOWBOXES

DEREK NIMMO

WARD LOCK

First published in Great Britain in 1990 by
Ward Lock, Artillery House, Artillery Row,
London SW1P 1RT England
125 East 23rd Street, Suite 300, New York 10010, USA
A Cassell imprint

Designed by Anita Ruddell
Photography by Jon Bouchier*
Horticultural consultant Barbara Haynes

*except for pictures on pages 20 and 26 by Michael
Warren, Photos Horticultural, and page 40 by
Andrew Lawson

Text typeset in Frutiger and Bodoni by Litho Link Ltd,
Welshpool, Powys, Wales
Printed and bound in Italy by Rotolito Lombarda

British Library Cataloguing in Publication Data
Nimmo, Derek, *1932–*
    Wonderful windowboxes.
    1. Window boxes. Plants. Cultivation
    I. Title
    635.9'65
    ISBN 0–7063–6846–0

PUBLISHER'S NOTE

Readers are requested to note that in order to make the text intelligible in both hemispheres, plant flowering times, etc. are generally described in terms of seasons, not months. The following table provides an approximate 'translation' of seasons into months for the two hemispheres.

NORTHERN HEMISPHERE			SOUTHERN HEMISPHERE
Mid-winter	=	January	= Mid-summer
Late winter	=	February	= Late summer
Early spring	=	March	= Early autumn
Mid-spring	=	April	= Mid-autumn
Late spring	=	May	= Late autumn
Early summer	=	June	= Early winter
Mid-summer	=	July	= Mid-winter
Late summer	=	August	= Late winter
Early autumn	=	September	= Early spring
Mid-autumn	=	October	= Mid-spring
Late autumn	=	November	= Late spring
Early winter	=	December	= Early summer

CONTENTS

PREFACE

I've always been a keen gardener, but it wasn't until a few years ago, and by accident, that I began to take a terribly serious interest in windowboxes. It all started one morning when I was woken by the sound of two strange voices in the garden. I couldn't think who they were so I put on my dressing-gown and hurried out, only to discover that my daughter had entered me for the Brighter Kensington and Chelsea garden competition, and the voices belonged to the judges. 'Have you filled in the form?' they asked, so I filled in the form and to my astonishment found myself in the finals. Being tolerably competitive I spent the whole summer weeding and pruning and planting the garden and the windowboxes until the judges (including the head gardener from Buckingham Palace) came round again. The upshot was that I was awarded a Highly Commended for both the garden and the windowboxes, and having got that I was automatically .entered for the finals of the following year's competition.

It so happened that for most of the following summer I was in Africa and my wife helped with the job of planting the windowboxes. Now I'm a Virgo, and Virgos like things neat and symmetrical and tidy. My wife, on the other hand, likes things asymmetrical and so while I was away she put lots of plants in the windowboxes in her own style. When I got back from Africa I was terribly miffed because I thought it was an awful mess. Which embarrasses me rather,

because that was the year I won the prize not only for the best windowbox in Kensington but also for the best windowbox in London. Since then I've relinquished the prize, but I still have windowboxes and still keep a lookout for new ideas.

Although attractive windowboxes are a pleasure anywhere, they are one of the great delights of town life. If you doubt me, I recommend a summer afternoon's walk around Kensington and Chelsea. Down almost every road you'll find the work of frustrated flat-dwellers who have perfected the art of gardening on their windowsills. It makes a terrific difference to our streets. Even the plainest houses and most boring shops, pubs and offices are transformed with a few windowboxes and hanging baskets.

Nowhere is this effect more obvious than in the City of London, with its grey pavements and huge grey buildings. I was stuck in a traffic jam outside the Mansion House only the other day (it was, coincidentally, the Mansion House where I went to receive my windowbox prizes) which gave me the opportunity to admire the masses of pink hydrangeas planted along the front of what is otherwise a rather forbidding building.

For discreet city style it's difficult to improve on these two neatly-clipped cubes of box. For something more outspoken one might consider a corkscrew spiral of box or a standard bay tree.

PREFACE

They broke up a wide expanse of greyish stone and made it look exceedingly jolly.

Despite that, it has to be said that there are still vast numbers of less-than-wonderful windowboxes dotting ledges all over the country. You know the kind of thing I mean – a few spindly, half-starved annuals in the summer and a bare expanse of dry earth the rest of the year. It doesn't have to be like this. With a little planning and know-how anyone can create windowboxes to be proud of. And that's where I hope this book will be useful, whether you're starting your window garden from scratch or looking for new ideas for existing boxes.

Among these pages you'll find many examples of plantings and styles for all seasons, with suggestions for many more. I have deliberately interpreted the term 'windowbox' widely so that in our photos we can take in a good variety of troughs and containers, not all of them on windowsills. Many of them are absolutely first-rate. Others are not quite so polished in their presentation but have been chosen because they illustrate bright and novel ideas or themes. I hope they'll inspire you to create wonderful windowboxes of your own and, in doing so, brighten your house or garden and give pleasure to everyone who passes by.

TOWN STYLE

ravelling around the country, always on the lookout for wonderful window-boxes, I've come to the conclusion that for town boxes a relatively formal style of planting is the best and most reliable. The multi-coloured cottage-garden look is fine in the country, particularly when it's used in profusion, but informal plantings look messy on the limited space of a city windowsill. In town the best windowboxes are those that make a dramatic impact, and they tend to be planted with one or two species in a well-chosen colour combination. Boring? It needn't be. A thriving two or three-coloured box can make a bolder, more positive statement than a container stuffed with a dozen competing varieties.

Single colour plantings — all white is a classic — look particularly agreeable. So do single shade plantings; a box planted in the yellow/orange/bronze spectrum will look warm and cheerful. Purposely contrived clashes — red and pink pelargoniums grouped together, for example — may achieve a sophisticated result. The important word here is *purposely*. The best town windowboxes are not thrown haphazardly together but planned with a definite theme in mind.

Limiting yourself to just a few varieties has an additional pay-off. As long as you choose plants that enjoy the same kind of growing conditions there's a good chance that they will all survive. The greater the number of varieties you cram into a single container, the greater the chance that some of them won't be able to cope.

Dust and pollution are two things that city dwellers take pretty much for granted, but the same cannot be said of all plants. Many tolerate pollution well; these include bulbs, camellias, polyanthus, sweet alyssum, roses, fuchsias, ivies and many evergreens. If you live near a busy road where plants have to contend with dust and lead from car exhausts, bear these in mind, and when choosing other plants look for the hardiest and most proven varieties.

AN EVERGREEN PLANTING

One of the simplest ways of having an attractive, low-maintenance windowbox display throughout the year is to use a permanent planting scheme like this one. The winter months would look so much better if more gardeners did this. There's nothing more depressing than walking along city streets on a gloomy winter day and seeing rows of empty, neglected boxes — or worse still, boxes filled with the dead remains of last summer's bedding plants. There's no excuse. It's possible to have an attractive easy-care windowbox all year round, and the easiest way is by using evergreens as a basic permanent planting.

This box, photographed in west London, is a good example of a year-round planting — simple to maintain and yet effective at softening what could be a stark-looking white house. Though none of the plants

WONDERFUL WINDOWBOXES

were in flower when we took the photograph, at other times the hebes and laurel will have flowers and berries. For those who like more colour it would be a simple task to add a few flowering plants or bulbs in season. A background of lush evergreens makes even the humblest annuals look classy. It is also possible to interplant the evergreens with perennials that stay in the box all year round. Turn to page 119 for suggestions for perennial plantings.

Most 'permanently' planted windowboxes like this one are good for two to three years if they are fed appropriately. After this the container will have to be emptied and the exhausted soil replaced with fresh compost. You will probably find that after this period, anyway, the plants are getting too big for the box and have to be removed. This method of planting young shrubs in windowboxes is an excellent way of growing them on to a decent size for the garden. And if you propagate from them, you can raise a new generation of small plants that will mature on your windowsill before joining their parents in the flowerbed.

Permanent planting requires some consideration. Shrubs and perennials are more expensive than bedding plants, and unlike bedding plants they're not over in a season. If you make the wrong selection you may end up wasting money or living with a windowbox you dislike; make the right choice and your boxes will be a pleasure throughout the year.

EVERGREENS

When choosing evergreens, look for a variety of leaf-shapes, forms and colours to create contrast and interest. These are some of the best.

Variegated japonicas are my first choice. Their leaves, splashed with yellow, are parti-

cularly attractive and almost indestructible. *Skimmia japonica* has plain green foliage, a neat growing habit, shiny leaves and produces white flowers in the late spring. Female plants follow this up with brilliant red berries in early autumn. Some people might turn their noses up at such a common choice, but the only reason one sees so many of these shrubs around is because they are easy to grow and offer such excellent value for money.

Euonymus makes a good foil to the above. 'Ovatus Aureus' has bold, glossy leaves with golden-yellow edges. It grows slowly and is tolerant of pollution and salt spray, which makes it ideal for a windowbox in a coastal position where a salty breeze could wreak havoc with more sensitive plants. *E. fortunei* 'Silver Queen' is just as easy to grow and has pretty cream-edged leaves that look particularly good as a backdrop to spring bulbs.

Dwarf conifers are fine windowbox material, their strong, upright shape contrasting well with the bushy habit of the other shrubs. Choose true dwarf varieties, which grow very slowly and may last several years.

Hebes are ideal windowbox plants. Perhaps the most practical is *H. pinguifolia* 'Pagei', a dwarf species with grey-blue leaves and spikes of white flowers. Other cultivars developed from *H. speciosa* have very dark, glossy leaves and stunning blue-purple flowers. Hebes are hardy and can tolerate hot, dry situations and salt spray.

Ivies are perhaps the most common of all windowbox plants, but not to be rejected because of that. Unique in providing year-round trailing and climbing cover and for their tolerance of most conditions, they're indispensable for clothing the front of a box or training up and around a window.

Try combining two varieties – one with a strong form and one with unusual colour – in the same box for a good visual contrast. For a bigger climber suitable for a large box or

A simple evergreen planting, easy to look after but pleasing nevertheless.

container, Persian ivy, *Hedera colchica*, is ideal. Its large leaves are most impressive and it can grow to a height of 30ft (10m). *H. Colchica* 'Dentata' is dark green while 'Variegata' has attractive yellow-edged leaves. Your local nursery will probably have a good selection of ivies on offer, but if you're unable to find what you're looking for in the garden section, check out the house-plants. Most ivies sold as houseplants are perfectly capable of surviving outdoors if planted in summer and given the opportunity to harden up before winter.

Cotoneaster dammeri evergreen grows very close to the ground and will drape over the front and sides of a windowbox in a dramatic way. It has small white flowers in early summer, which attract bees, followed by orange-red berries. *Co. microphyllus* is evergreen and has tiny leaves and large red fruits in autumn and winter.

Evergreen azaleas and rhododendrons must be grown in lime-free compost to make a spectacular display in the early summer. The *R. yakushimanum* hybrids, which grow to about 2ft (60cm), have dark green, leathery leaves and pale pink, pale peach or cream blossom. Your nursery should also be able to supply other dwarf hybrids. Azaleas and rhododendrons like shaded, damp conditions, which makes them suitable for gloomy north-facing windowsills or areas where there is poor light. They are thirsty plants and shallow rooting, so are only recommended for those prepared to keep up the watering. Their dark green foliage looks particularly good against bright green hostas, which share their love of damp shade.

Pieris formosa 'Forestii' gives good value in a large box. In spring it produces a mass of white flowers and as soon as these are over brilliant scarlet new leaves begin to unfold. Throughout the summer these turn pink and then cream until finally the whole plant assumes its glossy green winter colouring. Though this shrub can eventually reach well over 10ft (3m), its size may be limited by

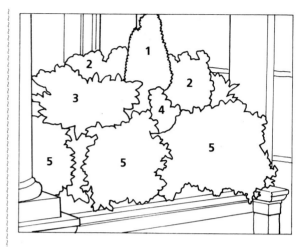

1 Dwarf conifer
2 Regal pelargonium
3 *Skimmia japonica*
4 Marguerite
5 Ivy

To the bare bones of this evergreen planting – dwarf conifer, Skimmia japonica and ivy – have been added a Regal pelargonium and marguerites.

pruning. The new scarlet foliage is suscept-ible to damage from late frosts, but on a sheltered window-ledge the danger is reduced. *P. formosa* looks particularly good when teamed with yellow-variegated plants or as a background for red and yellow annuals.

Box trees are used individually in pots for a classic windowsill display or as background material for a mixed planting. Dwarf forms such as 'Suffruticosa' can be trimmed into balls, cones or the spirals that seem to be very fashionable at present. Box is very slow growing, which is why it is expensive. On the plus side it is hardy and can be raised from cuttings, so having invested in it there's every chance of keeping it looking good.

Bay (*Laurus nobilis*) can be used like box to make slow-growing trees or as a shrubby addition to windowboxes.

Camellias thrive in large boxes or tubs for a year or two before their size requires them to be removed to the garden. Like rhododendrons they hate lime (so an ericaceous compost must be used) and enjoy shade, and although they look delicate they are very tolerant of air pollution. The x williamsii hybrids include cultivars that begin flowering as early as late autumn, providing colour during some of the dullest months of the year. When not in flower their shiny dark leaves are a good foil for other plants. On a sheltered window-ledge, protected from the wind and frost and in the shade, they can make an excellent specimen plant at the centre of a large box.

Ferns love damp, shady conditions and come in useful for gloomy basement windowsills. One of the best evergreens is the hart's-tongue, *Asplenium scolopendrium*, which has lovely strong green leaves with wavy edges. *Dryopteris filix-mas crispa cristata* grows to 15in (37cm) and has attractively crested fronds. The maidenhair spleenwort, *Adiantum venustum*, is also a suitable choice.

Yuccas have a strong, upright leaf shape that adds drama and architectural interest to any box. They are best for south-facing or sparsely-watered boxes. See page 24 for further details.

Rock plants such as sedums, saxifrages and houseleeks offer an exotic evergreen touch. Though at their best when planted in rock gardens, they be can used for contrast in ordinary windowboxes too. They should be planted at the front of the trough where their low-growing, spreading habit can be best appreciated.

Colourful cyclamen in white, red and pink create a patch of bright colour through the winter months. When interplanted with trailing ivies and evergreen conifers and laurels a truly stylish effect is achieved.

A WINTER PLANTING
WITH CYCLAMEN

When it comes to putting on a decent winter display, town gardeners have the advantage over their rural counterparts. Even in severe weather a city windowsill can be a surprisingly sheltered spot, set back out of the rain and protected from the worst of the wind by the surrounding buildings.

My favourite winter windowbox plants are cyclamen, which offer a splendid patch of colour through the darkest months of the year. In my experience they regularly flower right through from late autumn to early spring and I've seen them elsewhere valiantly flowering as late as late spring. Ideally they like semi-shaded positions and well-drained soil, but they are often tolerant of less than perfect conditions.

If you have a permanently planted box the corms can be placed directly into it, a couple of inches (centimetres) beneath the surface of the soil, from late summer onwards. If in late summer your boxes are brimming over with annuals which you intend to remove at the end of the season, it is better to plant the corms in pots and transfer them to the box when they are mature and will not be disturbed. It is easier still, particularly if you're living in a tiny town flat, to buy mature plants from the garden centre.

Cyclamen come in a variety of colours from white, through pale pink to bold crimsons and even purples, all of which make a wonderful splash of colour on a winter's day. All of them look fine against a background of dark evergreen foliage on winter-flowering heather and fronted by a mass of trailing ivy. In this box pink, white and red varieties have been planted with conifers and spotted laurel for a bold and cheerful combination.

In late winter or early spring they look effective when paired with some of the more delicate early bulbs. For a dazzling contrast plant the intensely blue squill, *Scilla sibirica*,

or *Chionodoxa luciliae* between dark red cyclamen. Those who prefer more subtle colouring might try *Chionodoxa luciliae* 'Pink Giant', available from specialist bulb suppliers, which has large pink flowers with white centres, or perhaps snowdrop hybrids (larger in stature and flower than the species) such as 'Magnet' or 'Sam Arnott'. Early-flowering crocuses are also attractive but have to be planted in full sun, otherwise the flowers will not open. Early crocuses grow only 3in (7cm) tall and usually appear in late winter. Try *C. chrysanthus* 'Skyline', with its distinctive soft blue flowers, or the pale yellow 'Cream Beauty'. Each bulb produces a number of flowers, so just a few of them planted along the front of a windowbox can give a surprisingly full show.

When the cyclamen have finished flowering, remove them from the windowbox and return them to pots where they can dry off and rest throughout the summer in a cool place, regaining their strength for next autumn. Treated this way, plants can last for many years.

A WINTER PLANTING
WITH HEATHERS

Small heathers of all kinds are excellent plants for windowboxes. They come in such a wide variety of colours and leaf-tints, including bronze, gold and silver, that it's possible to create a pleasing permanent display using nothing else. Perhaps the most useful heathers are the winter-flowering cultivars, *Erica carnea*, which flower at different times from late autumn through to early or mid-spring and provide colour at a difficult time of year. 'Springwood White', *E. gracilis*, which is a good pink, and 'Vivelli', with deep red flowers and foliage turning an attractive bronze in the winter, are particularly useful. 'Aurea' has bright golden foliage at its best in spring and summer, and pink flowers. These plants will grow into informal, bushy mounds between 6in (15cm) and 12in (30cm) high. Winter heathers are hardy and will flourish in

ordinary garden compost. Trim them back into neat mounds when they have finished flowering or remove from the box and place in the garden. The free-standing stone trough shown here combines deep pink heather and apricot-coloured pansies with neatly-trimmed box trees for a pleasing display that will last well into winter.

Summer-flowering heathers (*E. vagans*) are less commonly seen in containers because their flowering period coincides with that of most summer annuals. That said, they still make a useful contribution to a permanent planting scheme and different varieties will flower from mid-summer to mid-autumn. Particularly attractive is 'St Keverne', a rose-pink cultivar with dark green foliage. These summer-flowering heathers require acid soil; look for special lime-free ericaceous compost at the garden centre. Both summer and winter-flowering varieties like a sunny position and require little maintenance except for a quick trim when their flowers are over.

Heathers look particularly agreeable when close-planted with dwarf conifers and one could do far worse than create a permanently-planted display with a mixture of summer and winter-flowering cultivars interspersed with conifers. One of the smallest and most suitable conifers for a windowbox is the grey-green *Juniperus communis* 'Compressa', known as the Noah's Ark Juniper. It has a neat spire shape and will rarely grow more than 2ft (60cm) tall. It's best used with lower-growing plants and not with bigger shrubs, which tend to overshadow it. On a larger scale is *Chamaecyparis pisifera* 'Boulevard', which will reach a height of 15ft (5m) but, in its early years, is suitable for a windowbox. With its feathery blue-green foliage it makes a good colour contrast against darker or yellow-leaved plants. *C. lawsoniana* 'Minima Aurea' has a rounded

Heathers and pansies make excellent companions for winter windowboxes.

TOWN STYLE

shape and is a bright golden colour through-out the year – a good companion for red begonias or pelargoniums. The 'Ellwoodii' variety is spire-shaped but is not a true dwarf and will eventually have to be removed from the box.

The main problem with conifers is their tendency to 'burn' and develop dry brown patches. This can be caused by cold winters, chilling winds or drought. The solution is some kind of protection from the worst frosts and sufficient water throughout the year, winter as well as summer. I've also been told that anti-dessicants can be used to prevent burning. Sprayed on Christmas trees to prevent them from dropping their needles, they stop loss of water through the foliage. If you have had trouble with conifers in the past it may be worth a try.

AN EARLY SPRING PLANTING
WITH POLYANTHUS AND PANSIES

This box is one of several that decorate a rather bleak north-facing wall at the ent-rance of St Paul's Girls School in west London. They are planted and cared for by Valerie Jackson, one of the parents at the school. When it comes to windowboxes, Mrs Jack-son's gardening philosophy is to keep things simple. She likes to use evergreens to form the 'bones' of the box, here supplied by hebes and ivy, and interplant with seasonal colour. With these troughs on such public display, she wisely sticks to tried and trusted species that are able to take care of them-selves during the school holidays.

For winter colour she uses pansies (*Viola × wittrockiana*) – one or two survivors can just be seen in the picture. The winter-flowering strains such as 'Floral Dance' are hardy and will provide flowers from autumn right through to spring. The plain blue-violet strains look particularly good in a formal

A simple spring planting with hebes and polyanthus.

setting, but there are many other colours and varieties.

In late winter and early spring the pansies are supplemented or replaced by polyanthus, which will continue flowering into mid or even late spring. Polyanthus come in a broad spectrum of colours, from the pale pinks and creams seen here, to brilliant yellows, blues and reds and rich orange and bronze. They are best used in careful colour combinations – sunshine yellow, purple and scarlet for an eye-socking effect; pale pink and yellow against subtle grey-green foliage; or apricot, bronze or white as a foil to daffodils.

Polyanthus tend to flower most spectacu-larly in their first year. After that they grow in size but at the expense of their flowers. Put your old plants out in the garden when they are past their best and replace them with new ones each spring.

One of the first jobs when planting up most troughs is to ensure that the visible bits of the container are covered with ivy or other trailing plants. This one is so attractive, however, that the ivy has been placed at the sides, where it softens the outline of the trough against the grey wall behind and allows the detail of the stonework to be seen.

This particular trough, which depicts five disciples, comes from a company which specializes in reproducing antique stone containers and statues. Because this kind of container is so heavy, it's a good idea to check that your windowsills can take the strain before you purchase. It's also worth checking that the colour of the stone matches or complements the colour of the house. Stone containers can vary from light and dark grey to pale cream or the warm, golden tones of Bath stone. If you *do* make a mistake the colour of any new stone trough can be toned down with a coating of watery cement and peat, which encourages algae and moss to grow. Liquid manure works too. I've tried it myself on quite cheap concrete pots and they soon look wonderfully antique.

WONDERFUL WINDOWBOXES

Left. *Hyacinths not only look bright and cheerful during the winter months but also have a most agreeable scent. Here they're planted with brilliant blue scillas.*

Opposite. *These lead boxes are planted with marguerites in a Sissinghurst-influenced colour scheme.*

A SPRING PLANTING
WITH HYACINTHS AND SCILLAS

Hyacinths aren't, perhaps, the most elegant of plants, but their stubby stems and fragrant spikes of flowers are long-lasting and provide colour at a grey time of the year. Planted in the autumn they can be in bloom for winter and, in good conditions, will last a further two months until the later bulbs make their appearance. Hyacinths look best planted *en masse* in single-colour groups. This is important not just for aesthetic reasons but because bulbs of different colours flower at different times. There are many shades to choose from including pink, red, blue, yellow, white, cream and new colours such as an extraordinary salmony-orange shade.

To conceal their bare stems hyacinths should always be underplanted. Winter-flowering pansies are suitable for early-flowering varieties, polyanthus for later ones. But the best solution of all is to use small bulbs. Books are always recommending this method but one rarely sees it in practice — which is why this particular photograph was chosen. The pink hyacinths have been planted behind brilliant blue *Scilla sibirica*, which flowers in mid-spring and creates a

really bold splash of blue. Each small bulb produces several stems of flowers, so only a few are needed to produce a good display. Scilla are best planted in the summer or early autumn. Like hyacinths they are happiest in full sun but will tolerate light shade. Treat both species as for other bulbs, digging them up and storing them throughout the summer. This box would, in my opinion, have looked even better if the plastic had been covered with plenty of ivy.

Other bulbs suitable for underplanting include *Chionodoxa luciliae*, which have bright blue flowers on 6in (15cm) stems. These plants have very little foliage which means that the flowers are shown to best effect. *Iris reticulata*, early crocuses, snowdrops and grape hyacinths (*Muscari armeniacum*) all make good companions for hyacinths and, for that matter, other taller bulbs.

A SUMMER PLANTING
WITH MARGUERITES

These west-London windowboxes grace the study of a friend of mine, Gyles Brandreth. Gyles is not, I have to say, the best gardener I have ever met — not, I hasten to add, from lack of interest but because of his hectic

working schedule. When I telephoned and asked him if his new boxes were ready to be photographed he assured me they were. But when the photographer arrived a few days later he found that the marguerites hadn't been dead-headed for some time. 'If you don't look at the dead bits, they're fine,' commented Brandreth, undaunted.

There's nothing more summery and charming than a windowbox packed with daisies but, as this tale reveals, they do need plenty of attention. For this reason marguerites and most other daisies are avoided by professional gardeners who make up and maintain windowboxes for their customers — and they are also best avoided by anyone who doesn't have ten minutes most evenings to pick off the dead flowerheads before they go brown. This task isn't as unpleasant as it sounds, particularly if, like me, you develop the skill of dead-heading with one hand, leaving the other free to hold a glass of sherry.

Dead-heading is one of the prime rules of all successful gardeners, and it's even more necessary when you're gardening on a small scale. One or two dead flowers in a garden will go unnoticed, but they're quite enough to ruin the effect of a windowbox. The other reason for dead-heading is that it encourages new flowers to grow. By trimming plants back from time to time you can actually extend the flowering season and produce more blooms.

According to Gyles, when this box was planted from scratch in the early summer the intention was to give it a 'Sissinghurst feel' by keeping it to a white, pale green and greyish colour scheme based on the colours used in Vita Sackville-West's famous silver and white garden at Sissinghurst in Kent. The marguerites were interplanted with white petunias, *Helichrysum petiolatum*, with its furry silver-grey leaves, and the lime-green/grey form 'Limelight'. The corners of the boxes are planted with low-growing 'mystery plants' picked up unnamed and cheaply at a north London nursery. They look suspiciously like variegated cotoneasters and it will be interesting to see how they develop. Though the Brandreths don't want to cover the front of the boxes completely, they also planted another trailing variegated grey-green mystery plant with fleshy leaves. Marguerites and petunias both love sun and well-drained conditions. The Brandreths' windowsills face west but are quite heavily shaded by trees, so this is not the ideal situation for these plants.

The windowboxes themselves are made of lead and were custom-built to fit the ledges.

Boxes like this are ideal for big windows because they look so substantial and weighty. They are a serious investment, but they will last for many years and become more attractive with age. Being so deep, they can take much larger plants than mass-produced containers, a fact which the Brandreths intend to exploit. Once this first season is over the boxes will be emptied and permanently planted with shrubs that will better appreciate the conditions.

A SUMMER PLANTING
WITH HYDRANGEAS

The windowboxes in this picture are completely hidden beneath a mass of white mophead hydrangeas (known technically as Hortensias to distinguish them from the Lacecap variety) and a curtain of trailing ivies to create a quite breathtaking summer display. In spring the house looks equally pleasant, with drifts of daffodils beneath the windows. These are truly wonderful windowboxes all year round!

White hydrangeas always look sophisticated and they perfectly balance a formal red-brick town house like this. Given a sunny position and moist soil they will thrive throughout the summer as long as they are not allowed to dry out. They are therefore recommended only to those who are dedicated and reliable waterers, or who have an automatic watering system.

Automatic systems are a great boon to the gardener who wants to grow an ambitious display and yet can't guarantee regular watering by hand. Most systems consist of a computerized timing device which can be attached to a garden tap. This box of tricks is then pre-set to turn the water on and off several times a day, rather in the manner of a central heating boiler control. The water flows down a main hosepipe to which can be added a series of flexible perforated tubes that come in a variety of shapes and sizes to service a considerable number of containers. Once they have been positioned on the soil these narrow pipes are soon lost among the foliage. When the automatic timer switches on, water circulates through the system and either drips directly onto the soil or creates a mist of moisture.

There's a house I stay at regularly in Melbourne, Australia, which is equipped with a most thorough sprinkler system that goes off at two o'clock in the morning without any warning at all. If you come home later after a jolly night out on the town you can be drenched in a tropical downpour as you cross the garden to the house.

This kind of system is invaluable for anyone who travels a great deal or the elderly gardener (like myself) who finds it difficult to run around with watering-cans or a hose. The prices for the basic 'computer' attachment, plus the extra costs of the hoses and other accessories may seem expensive, but if your boxes and containers are planted up with costly perennials and shrubs (such as the hydrangeas in this picture) it is not an unreasonable investment.

If the idea of a computerized watering system doesn't attract you, there are other less high-tech ways of watering your windowboxes. A friend of a friend has a home-made, deeply low-tech, method based on a length of copper piping obtained from a plumbing supply shop. The pipe is sealed at one end, perforated at regular intervals and attached to the balcony just above the windowboxes. It then runs through a neatly-drilled hole in the house wall into the kitchen, where it joins the mains water supply and is controlled by a tap under the sink. When the tap is turned on, water simply drips or sprays from the holes in the pipe. Of course this system isn't fully automated and someone has to be around to turn it on and off again, but it saves time and energy.

Splendid curtains of ivy fall from beneath white hydrangeas.

AN EXOTIC SUMMER PLANTING

This unusual box has a rather spiky, exotic air about it thanks to the yuccas and urn plants (*Aechmea fasciata*) at its centre. It may not be to the taste of those who like traditional summer flowers, but for anyone looking for an alternative to the usual pelargoniums and fuchsias, it's certainly worth considering.

Urn plants are usually seen indoors, but there's no reason why they shouldn't do well in a sheltered spot during a hot, dry summer – as this box proves. When they're three or four years old they produce these intriguing pink flower heads covered in spiny bracts. So long as they don't get too cold or wet, these flowers remain attractive for about six months – quite long enough to see you through the summer months. In autumn they can be removed and taken into the conservatory or used as pot plants. Almost as commanding as their flowers are the broad, leathery-textured leaves. They can grow up to 2 ft (60cm) long and are crossed with silver-grey bands.

Planted behind these are two yuccas, their upright, spiky foliage giving the box extra height. Yuccas are good 'architectural' plants with strong shapes; they provide instant drama, whatever their setting. They also offer some privacy to the occupants of the house without completely obscuring the view or the light, which is worth bearing in mind if you're bothered by passers-by peering in at your windows.

Both the urn plants and the yuccas thrive in warm, sunny conditions in well-drained soil that is only moderately watered. They are a good combination for a south-facing windowsill and require little attention apart from occasional watering and monthly feeding. The urn plants seem to do particularly well if you apply liquid feed to the rosette from which the flower stalk grows, as well as watering it into the soil around the roots. In a sheltered spot the yuccas will be hardy enough to flourish throughout the year.

Yuccas and urn plants make an unusual alternative to traditional summer annuals. Both will flourish on a sunny windowsill, but the busy lizzies would prefer a little shade.

1 Yucca
2 Urn plant
3 Busy lizzie
4 Variegated ivy

Pink and grey plantings are always attractive, and here the pink of the urn plants is picked up by the busy lizzies spilling down the front of the box. Even the variegated ivy beneath has been well-chosen to complement the grey-green theme and balance the box.

TOWN STYLE

A SUMMER PLANTING WITH MINIATURE ROSES AND CLEMATIS

Miniature roses, like the 'Pixie' rose shown here, make an attractive display in early and mid-summer and often flower a second time in the autumn. They are best planted in a sunny position in spring in well-drained compost and apart from dead-heading and pruning require little maintenance.

Like other roses, miniatures do best when they have been well-manured. As well-rotted farm manure is both difficult to come by and not always a practical proposition in town, you could use one of the concentrated organic manures available either by mail order (see advertisements in gardening magazines) or from your garden centre. Though still somewhat smelly, they come in dehydrated and compacted forms that are relatively easy to handle. If messing about with manure is quite out of the question, roses will respond to fortnightly doses of one of the many liquid feeds available.

On the subject of roses, a couple of years ago I was privileged to have a rose named after me by Mattocks of Oxford. The rose was introduced at the Chelsea Flower Show and on the day I rushed to the tent and picked up the catalogue to read my entry. 'DEREK NIMMO' it said, 'Derek Nimmo in its youth is breathtakingly beautiful but rather prone to mildew.' It ended up with 'Derek Nimmo has vigorous bushy growth and a fine upright stem,' which at my age was distinctly comforting.

Another friend of mine, actress Dulcie Grey, had a similar surprise when she saw herself listed in a rose-grower's catalogue. 'DULCIE GREY:', went the entry, 'not very good for bedding but fine up against a wall.'

Personally I'm not very keen on miniature roses in containers. Too often they look spindly (those in this picture are an exception) and in the winter and spring they have nothing to offer. They're best removed each autumn and over-wintered in pots. Prune them back before replacing them in the windowboxes the following spring. Better still, remove the entire box from the windowsill in autumn and replace it with another with Christmas cherries or cyclamen. Keep the roses in a sheltered outdoor spot and prune gently in early spring to encourage new growth. By late spring or early summer they should be ready to go back on to the windowsill once more.

This may seem an extravagant way of going about things, but having two sets of windowboxes makes it so much easier to keep up a good year-round display of colour, particularly when you are using perennials. The best system of all is to build a permanent wooden box on your windowsill and to have two sets of 'liners' – these need be nothing more than cheap plastic containers. This way you can leave your summer perennials undisturbed in a quiet corner of the garden over the winter and still have constant colour on your window-ledges.

Propagating from miniature roses couldn't be easier and will ensure that each season you have new plants to replace any that fail. Take half-ripe cuttings in summer, trim to about 3in (7cm), dip in hormone rooting powder (this is not essential but does help) and insert in a pot filled with equal measures of peat and sharp horticultural sand. This method works for many shrubby plants although some (lavender, for example) seem to root better if a heel of older wood is left attached to the cutting.

Miniature roses shown at their best against a background of purple clematis.

A SUMMER PLANTING
IN BLUE AND WHITE

The idea of a blue and white windowbox sounded rather cool and clinical before I saw this pleasant planting at a location in west London. My suspicion that we'd find nothing but lobelia was banished. This discreet colour combination seemed ideally suited to the subdued decoration of the house – more in keeping with its dark green paint and trailing greenery than brilliant pinks and reds. Once again it admirably demonstrates the virtues of following a limited colour scheme.

When it was originally planted up in late spring the box was centred around two lavender-blue scabious ('Clive Greaves'). Though rarely seen in windowboxes these can make attractive focal plants, with large flowers on long stems that give height to the planting. As long as they are dead-headed regularly scabious will usually flower non-stop from early summer through to late autumn. On this occasion, unfortunately, they did not. By late mid-summer they had stopped flowering and were looking less than healthy. They were quickly cut back, removed from the boxes and replaced with lavender (*Lavandula angustifolia* 'Hidcote', a purple-blue dwarf variety) to give height and scent. The rest of the box is filled with blue and white lobelia, petunias, purple-blue trailing verbena, trailing and standard white pelargoniums (geraniums) and campanula, with ivies with strong creamy-white variegation. From one corner of the box climbs a Morning Glory (*Ipomoea*), found growing wild in the garden and resourcefully popped into position so that its blue flowers, which appear at their best in the morning, could twine through the honeysuckle around the window and complete the theme. Unfortunately, when this plant came into bloom it revealed itself to be not the standard blue variety but pink. That set-back aside, it's an excellent idea to grow climbing plants from windowboxes to frame the window, and annuals such as the Morning Glory grow as profusely as weeds. Just train them up a string or round an existing climber and stand back.

1 Lavender
2 White pelargoniums
3 White campanula
4 Purple petunias
5 Felicia
6 Lobelia and trailing verbena
7 Ivy

Cool blues, purples and whites are fresh and informal against the subdued dark paint of the window-frames and the climber-covered walls.

TOWN STYLE

TOWN STYLE

A BALCONY
PLANTED FROM CUTTINGS

The boxes along this balcony had only been planted for a few months when we photographed them, and though they look good now, in a year or two they will make an even more spectacular cascade of colour. They're tended by Catherine Horwood, a very dedicated and knowledgeable Hampstead gardener who modestly describes herself as 'semi-professional'.

One of the fascinating things about her terrace of boxes is that most of the plants came from cuttings. As she explained, there's a very varied selection: 'I though you might be interested to have the names of *some* of the plants in my balcony boxes. There are geranium (pelargonium) 'Deacon Lilac Mist', unknown single coral ivy-leaved pelargoniums, white, pink and 'Speckles' varieties of pelargonium, *Helichrysum petiolatum* and variegated and yellow forms of the same, *Felicia amelloides* and a variegated form, myrtle (*Myrtus communis*), wall germander (*Teucrium chamaedrys*), *Dianthus*, variegated sage, lobelia and various petunias. This, of course, doesn't include the pots at the side!

'Virtually all of them were grown from cuttings, certainly the ivy-leaf pelargoniums and the helichrysums. Some plants (the felicia especially) came from cuttings I took in Spain a couple of years ago. I didn't buy anything from nurseries.'

This is a proud boast that very few gardeners of my acquaintance can make. Small wonder that Catherine carries off prizes at her local horticultural society, including a trophy donated by Sydney Arrobus, another Hampstead gardener whose own prize-winning terrace is featured in this

Trailing pelargoniums and helichrysum are used here to break up the lines of a new conservatory and terrace and integrate them with the garden below.

31

book (see page 49).

This terrace is proof that you don't need to spend a fortune on planting up your windowboxes. Most plants suitable for containers can be propagated very easily from cuttings obtained from friends and neighbours. Ivy, for example, is easily raised from cuttings in autumn or spring. Cut off a length just below a leaf joint, remove a few of the lower leaves and insert into a pot containing a mixture of equal quantities of peat and sharp horticultural sand or cutting compost. To propagate pelargoniums take stem cuttings in spring, summer or autumn. Cut them just below a leaf joint and remove the lower leaves with a clean, sharp knife. Dip the stem into hormone rooting powder, tap off the excess and insert round the edge of a pot containing equal measures of peat and cutting compost or sharp sand. Stand in a propagator or cover with a polythene bag until rooting has taken place. Helichrysum and many other common windowbox plants can be raised in exactly the same way. Remember always to take cuttings from healthy, vigorous plants; diseased or unhealthy plants should be discarded.

Some plants are true annuals and have to be grown from scratch each year but others – like the pelargoniums, for example – can be cut back to about half their size at the end of the season, potted up and overwintered in a frost-free garden shed. When they are replanted next year they'll have a head start on the new cuttings and will achieve an even more impressive display than the previous year.

A PLANTING WITH DAHLIAS

By the time dahlias come into their own in mid-summer most windowboxes will have been planted up for perhaps two months, which probably explains why one sees so few of these plants outside the flower border. It may also be due to the fact that, in my experience, gardeners either love dahlias or hate them. Those who appreciate them love their showy blooms, neat symmetry and brilliant colours – the very reasons why those gardeners who prefer informal, understated plantings hate them so much.

I'm not going to join the debate, but people do find that dwarf dahlias can make a very useful contribution to windowbox displays. They bloom from mid-summer, some varieties even earlier, and unless they are in an exposed position will still be flowering at the end of the autumn. Unlike many annuals which grow straggly and unkempt-looking towards the end of the summer, dahlias remain neat and compact throughout the season. Their foliage is dense and tidy even if, heaven forbid, there's a temporary lack of blooms. And when they *are* in flower dahlias provide a splash of intense colour. The best, perhaps, are the brilliant scarlets and pinks; zinging oranges and yellows are already well covered by French or African marigolds.

Our example is interesting because of the combination of unusual foliage colours. At the back of the box are two shaggy blue-green *Chamaecyparis pisifera* 'Boulevard', flanked at each end by impressive bronze-leaved busy lizzies of the kind commonly used for terrace tubs and conservatories. They have the height and mass to match the conifers; smaller plants might be dwarfed by them. These large busy lizzies will, I'm sure, be taken indoors for the winter and returned to the garden in spring. Tucked between the conifers is a Regal pelargonium, while a row of semi-double golden dahlias provide the lightness in what could have been rather a heavy-looking box. A number of different ivies, including an attractive spidery one, complete the planting.

Dahlias require dedicated dead-heading, especially in wet weather when their flowers

Dahlias make an interesting contrast to the dark leaves of the giant busy lizzies and the unusual blue-green of large conifers.

can go brown very quickly. They are also, if my experience is anything to go by, very popular with slugs and snails. Slug-hunting is one of my favourite blood-sports. I first became deeply interested in it when I was in a play with Hugh Williams who had a house next door to Lady Macmillan's. She was a great nocturnal gardener and used to go round the garden with a miner's lamp on a helmet, catching the slugs as they came out, so I adopted the same method and started slug-hunting at night when I got back from the theatre. I can recommend the thrill of the chase and the kill when slugging at night. I finish the slugs off by dropping them in a jar of pellets. They eat themselves to death, and, I presume, die happy.

A TOPIARY BOX

This example of topiary is set along the top of a high wall in a street just off Berkeley Square in London. It's a simple but very effective way of making a feature of the wall and linking it with the boxes at the windows of the building. Balls and cones of clipped box alternate with each other, while beneath trails a heavy curtain of ivy. Even the ivies have been carefully chosen to give a good range of leaf shape, size, colour and growth habit. The result is frightfully elegant, and because box grows so slowly it should require little in the way of maintenance. Remember, however, that after the second year the top layer of compost should be replaced annually to ensure further growth.

If this kind of thing is too restrained for your taste, I've seen small box trees 2ft (60cm) or so high being sold in nurseries already cut to traditional – and not-so-traditional – shapes. There were cones and spirals and peacocks, as one might expect,

Elegant topiary balls and cones top a wall in Mayfair in London. Note how the ivies have been carefully planted to create a pattern of their own.

and also a teddy bear and a squirrel. They could be used in individual pots at the sides of a large window, and I'm sure the bear and the squirrel would go down particularly well on a child's windowsill.

As an alternative to box, consider bay, which can be clipped into simple shapes. Or how about growing ivy over a purpose-built frame or even one made of chicken wire, something I've noticed on visits to America? Working this way one can fairly quickly obtain large and surprisingly accurate shapes – a kind of living sculpture for the garden.

My personal encouter with living sculpture came when I was doing a programme called *Just a Nimmo*. One episode was all about impermanent art, which included flower-arranging. Kenneth Turner, a very well-known London florist, came on it and pre-sented me with a koala bear made on a wire frame covered with moss. It was live on the programme so I thanked him very much for it but couldn't think why on earth he'd given me a koala bear. So when we'd finished I asked him why a koala and he said, 'Well, you are Australian, aren't you?' I'm not, actually, I'm English.

Anyway, a large moss-covered koala isn't the king of thing one can do that much with, so we put it in the garden – and rolling koalas *do* gather moss, I assure you, because it sprouted and grew quite spectacularly until the spring. Then the birds started looking for material to build their nests. Within a week it was pecked bare and all we had was the metal frame. So take my advice, use ivy for living sculptures by all means, but don't, whatever you do, use moss.

AN AUTUMN/WINTER PLANTING WITH CHRISTMAS CHERRIES

If you've had trouble growing Christmas cherries (*Solanum capsicastrum*) indoors, take heart – and put them out on your windowsill. They may hate hot, dry, centrally-heated air but they'll thrive in a cool, sunny outdoor position where they are protected from frosts. They are an ideal choice for south-facing sheltered windowboxes from mid-autumn through to spring. Though they are not hardy and are unlikely to survive a very severe winter, I have seen them looking very agreeable, still with orange berries, in late spring.

Their shrubby, compact shape looks good against a background of darker evergreens, but be sure to give them sufficient light or they will become leggy and sparse. For what might be termed a 'warm autumnal glow', combine Christmas cherries with rust or bronze-coloured pot chrysanthemums. Yellow chrysanthemums create an altogether sunnier effect, demonstrated in our picture. The tall, architectural shape of the bronze-toned yucca gives the whole box impressive height and is balanced by the heavy curtain of ivy. To keep them looking healthy, feed the plants with a liquid fertilizer every two weeks. It's surpris-ing how many people, more used to plants that bloom in the summer months, assume that winter flowering plants don't require feeding or watering. They do, of course, and in the case of the Christmas cherry you will be repaid with plenty of marble-sized fruits and glossy foliage.

When the time comes to replace them, remove the plants from the windowbox and repot them with new potting compost. Trim them back to about half their size and put them outside, still in their pots, for the summer months. By the autumn they should be ready to produce another display for the windowbox.

One final note: the small orange berries of the Christmas cherry are enticing but are not, unfortunately, edible. Do, therefore, make sure that the boxes are safely out of reach of children.

Christmas cherries combined with bold yellow chrysanthemums echo the traditional colours of autumn.

COUNTRY STYLE

If the best city plantings are formal and restrained, the opposite is true of windowboxes in rustic settings. With a picturesque cottage as a backdrop, anything goes. A riot of rampant, clashing colours; a dozen different species all blooming together in one container; extraordinary boxes — pillar-box red, rustic wood, shell-covered . . . . All those things that are potential problems in town can look wonderful if planted with abandon in the country.

It's easy to assume that informal abundance can be easily obtained by throwing a random selection of plants into any old container, but achieving a truly charming effect is as much an art as formal town planting. The same rules still apply, whether in town or country. Windowboxes and their contents should be chosen to suit the architecture of the house and the lifestyle of the occupants.

Look out, if you live in the country, for interesting containers. Chimney pots, old stone sinks, hay racks, chipped china basins, old buckets and watering cans, battered saucepans, even a big old teapot, can make attractive containers on or beneath a window-ledge if they are used with style. But if you do decide to use this sort of unusual container, make sure that the plants inside them look absolutely first-rate. A rusty churn or old barrel full of glorious, healthy blooms looks wonderful, but the same stunning container packed with wilting or dead plants is an abysmal eyesore.

Wit is vital when using unusual containers. On a trip to Bermuda I passed a house where the drive was lined with old loos, all of them abundantly planted. One on its own might have looked rather quaint, but dozens of them together were a *tour de force*. More recently on a visit to Brighton I noticed a seafront house with windowboxes decorated with shells — just right for a seaside home. And the other day I passed a country garage where all the windowsills had on them containers made of oil cans, still with the manufacturer's name and logo intact. They were planted with brilliant red pelargoniums and dark blue lobelia and looked not just exceeding jolly but also appropriate to the setting.

A SPRING PLANTING
WITH MINIATURE BULBS

A windowbox filled with miniature daffodils and glowing polyanthus makes a bright start to the gardening year. There's something delightfully informal about miniature bulbs in a country-style trough. Ordinary daffodils tend to look rather solemn and regimented in windowboxes, but miniatures sown in clumps, as here, have a haphazard feel.

Miniature daffodils (or narcissi as they are known in the bulb catalogues) are easy to

Cheerful miniature daffodils and multi-coloured polyanthus under a kitchen window.

grow and, if you choose the tougher hybrids, will be successful in most conditions. The catalogue I have in front of me at the moment lists a hundred different varieties. Perhaps the best and most reliable is 'Tete-a-Tete', which grows 6in (15cm) high and usually makes its appearance in late winter. It flowers prolifically over a long period and is a strong golden colour. Slightly larger are 'February Gold' and 'February Silver', each 12in (30cm) tall and acknowledged for their long flowering period. If they are too large for your requirements, try something more unusual — and, consequently, more expensive. *N. rupicola*, or one of its varieties, grows only 3in (7cm) tall, has scented pale yellow flowers and is guaranteed to intrigue.

Miniature daffodils are particularly useful for planting in basements or areas where there's restricted light. Because they are smaller they don't become as leggy as larger varieties as they grow up to the light. It's important to plant bulbs really deep, as deep as 6in (15cm), so that they have some support if they grow tall.

As an alternative to daffodils, why not plant *Iris reticulata*? These small, bulbous irises are easy to grow and less delicate than they appear. The deep lemon-yellow *I. danfordiae* grows 6in (15cm) high and in a sheltered spot comes into flower soon after Christmas. Combine it with snowdrops at the front of the box and tulips behind. Another very early iris is 'Katharine Hodgkin', an unusual creamy colour with blue and pale yellow tones that is guaranteed to cause comment. By late winter the blue and purple iris are in flower. Look for *I. histrioides* 'George' or *I. reticulata* 'Cantab' (Cambridge blue) or 'Pauline', which has dusky violet-pink flowers.

Both *Iris reticulata* and narcissi should be planted from late summer onwards. They like fertile, reasonably well-drained compost and benefit from a sprinkling of bonemeal or a general-purpose fertilizer. Put them in a sunny, sheltered spot where they will get full light. When they finish flowering, leave the foliage as long as possible before trimming back. When the time comes to plant summer annuals, remove the bulbs from the windowbox and put them somewhere dark and dry — the airing cupboard or a corner of the garden shed is ideal. Replant at the end of the summer for more flowers the following spring.

A SPRING PLANTING
WITH TULIPS AND WALLFLOWERS

Elegant tulips nodding above brightly-coloured and scented wallflowers (*Cheiranthus*) are a traditional spring combination. Wallflowers are useful windowbox plants, flowering from mid-spring to early summer in a wide range of colours, through sharp yellows and vibrant reds to more subtle bronzes, apricots and pinks. Though they are traditionally used with tulips, providing ground cover, the dwarf varieties also look good on their own if they are massed tightly in a single-colour group.

When it comes to tulips the container gardener is quite spoiled for choice. If the container is a large one, like this stone trough, you can use taller 'Cottage' varieties with their big flowers and tough stems that can grow to 2ft (60cm) and more. They come in a wide range of colours, from plain scarlets and yellows to subtle, variegated varieties such as 'Artist', a combination of pale green, apricot and salmon pink. I have noticed that these vari-tinted forms, the Viridiflora and the frilly Parrot tulips, have become increasingly popular in recent years. Also suitable for large containers are members of the Darwin group of tulips, including 'William Pitt', a strong red. More delicate in form are the lily-flowered tulips which have long, outward-arching petals and a distinct 'urn' shape. Best

Opposite. *A traditional combination of tulips and wallflowers is totally in keeping with this picturesque stone trough.*

of the lot is 'China Pink', a deep pink flower with a paler interior. Though they look fragile these tulips are weather resistant and surprisingly robust.

For smaller windowboxes it is difficult to beat *Tulipa praestans* 'Fusilier', as red as a guardsman's tunic and measuring only 8in (20cm) tall. Each bulb produces between three and five flowers which are long-lasting and guarantee a vivid display. *T. praestans* 'Unicum' is bright scarlet like 'Fusilier' but each petal is edged with pale yellow. Also good is *T. fosteriana* 'Cantata', a vermillion-red with shiny dark green foliage. This looks particularly pleasing when interplanted with grape hyacinths. The foliage of most tulips is of secondary importance to the flower, but for something rather different look for dwarf forms of *T. greigii*, which have green leaves mottled with purple and brown. Some people find these plants rather busy, but once the flowers are over the leaves make an interesting feature – which is more than can be said of most tulips. Many of the botanical tulips or tulipa have lovely centres and are specially attractive if viewed from above. They're ideal for a low trough, where the full complexity of their colours and forms can be seen.

Kaufmanniana tulips are a particularly early variety, appearing in late winter and early spring. Their flowers open wide, hence their common name of water-lily tulips. Measuring between 5 and 8in (12 and 20cm) in height, most varieties are creamy white, flushed or mottled with pink or yellow at the base of each flower. Also worth considering are *T. tarda*, which form rosettes of foliage with up to five pointed-petalled white flowers with bright yellow centres. Being so low-growing, these are ideal for planting along the edge of a container with taller tulips at the back.

Tulips are best planted in early winter, 4in (10cm) deep and at least 4in (10cm) apart. They like well-drained soil and a sunny, south-facing position with good light;

they're definitely not recommended for basements or other gloomy areas. For a really good display plant two or three varieties that come into flower from early to late spring. This will ensure a constant supply of flowers until early summer. When the flowers are over allow the leaves to die down, then dig up the bulbs and store them in a warm, dark place until they are required in six months' time.

A BUSY LIZZIE BOX

No plant gives better value in windowboxes and containers, in my opinion, than the ubiquitous busy lizzie (or *Impatiens* as they are technically known). Until the hardy forms of this plant were introduced I often used petunias as the basic bedding in a box. They were reliable but rather straggly growers with occasional intervals between flowers and much prone to disease. Neither of those complaints can be held against busy lizzies. Mine are in flower by late spring and are usually still going strong in mid and even late autumn, with never a day without a profusion of colour. They have a pleasingly neat growth habit, don't seem to attract pests and come in a range of colours to suit all tastes. They also prefer a shady aspect which makes them ideal for difficult north and east-facing window-ledges and for basements. Most important of all, they never need dead-heading!

As proof of their sterling qualities I offer you a picture of the windowbox in the basement of my own home in London. This area gets very little sun and has to be planted with care – bulbs don't grow well down here, for example. But for busy lizzies it's no problem at all. My boxes are also planted up with conifers and two lobelias, the magenta and pale blue varieties.

I like these bright colours down in the

Brilliant busy lizzies are my favourite plants for summer windowboxes.

basement but for something softer try *Impatiens* Super Elfin F1 Hybrid 'Blush', which has large pale pink flowers each with a crimson centre. These would look effective with a background of silver plants such as *Senecio maritimus*. 'Florette Coral' is an apricot colour, good against shiny dark green foliage. For something altogether showier try one of the Double F1 hybrids such as 'Double Confection', available in a variety of colours and producing double flowers more than 1in (2cm) across. *Balsam* Extra Dwarf Tom Thumb is a strain of *I. balsamina* and has even larger double flowers. Despite its name it grows up to 12in (30cm) high. All these plants can be grown from seed if they are not available from your local nursery.

Two quick tips: first, when buying potted specimens select them already in flower. There can be a huge variation in shades of red or pink, for example, and buying plants already in flower is the only way of ensuring that they all match or clash as intended. The second tip, which applies to all plants and not just busy lizzies, is to choose a colour that shows up well against the background and the box. The importance of this came home to me when I saw a white wooden box filled with white busy lizzies and campanula against a white wall. I'm sure the owner thought it would be very smart, but in practice the flowers so merged with everything around them as to be practically invisible. Another mistake, in my opinion anyway, was a terracotta windowbox filled with red and pink busy lizzies and situated on the sill of a red-brick house. Container, brickwork and flowers were all so glaringly at odds that it almost hurt to look at them.

Though most people treat busy lizzies as annuals they will over-winter quite happily if kept in a frost-free spot. The best idea is to lift them at the end of the season and keep them indoors on a semi-shaded windowsill. Growing them on like this not only saves money but means good large plants the following spring. Propagation is easy – just take a few careful cuttings from favourite plants – so once you have a few plants there's no need to go out and buy more. As I said to begin with, busy lizzies are tremendous value for money!

A PLANTING WITH PETUNIAS

In recent years the popularity of petunias has been usurped by newer species that can offer crisper blooms and tidier growth, but they still make an excellent show, as you can see from this box. Nothing can really rival petunias for depth of colour, from inky-purple and velvety crimson to the more delicate shades of pink and lavender. The fancier varieties such as 'Hoolahoop', which has brilliant red petals frilled with white, or 'Starship', with bold white star-shaped markings, make cheerful single-variety plantings and look especially good with a backdrop of dark evergreen leaves. Other cultivars (try 'Daddy') have distinctive veined effects and graduated colour. My penchant for keeping things simple means that I'm not very keen on the double varieties. Petunias are generally more disease resistant and weatherproof than they once were, but the white strains are still susceptible to rain damage and in the past I have had problems with wireworm.

Pink and blue colour combinations always look attractive, whether they're subtle pastel shades as here or the sizzling hot colours that one sees so often in Mediterranean countries. Cerise and purple petunias would make a strong statement; add some crimson flowers too, and you end up with a wonderful 'hot' feel.

Also playing its part in this box, as in so many others, is that old favourite lobelia. It's something of a cliché, but only because it's

Pastel petunias complement the pale colours of this Cotswold art gallery. Note how the grey-green of their foliage echoes the green of the paintwork.

such a reliable and useful plant. Most people still go for the blue shades, but white, strong pinks and deep reds are also available. 'Cambridge Blue' (pale blue) and 'Crystal Palace' (dark blue) are the traditional favourites, but for something a bit different try 'Red Cascade' (deep pink to reddish purple flowers and a trailing habit) or 'Rosamund' (cherry-red with a white centre). Incidentally, when you next choose lobelia you might like to bear in mind some advice from Jilly Cooper in her book *Class*. Oxford blue, she says, is terribly vulgar, but Cambridge blue is okay!

A TROUGH PLANTING WITH CALCEOLARIAS AND FUCHSIAS

This frightfully attractive trough and hanging basket display was photographed in Stratford-upon-Avon. Windowboxes aren't necessarily practical or in keeping with a period house like this, but the free-standing trough of weathered timber is entirely in harmony with its surroundings – and so is the planting.

Though a good variety of multi-coloured plants have been used, they've been set out in orderly horizontal rows. The effect is picturesque but tidy and ordered, complementing the formal town setting of the house. At the back, providing height, are red pelargoniums; notice how their variegated leaves contribute to the colourful effect. Other pelargoniums with good leaf coloration are 'Mrs Parker', which has pale pink flowers and leaves edged with cream, or the spectacular 'Mrs Henry Cox', a showy plant whose pink flowers seem quite secondary to its tri-colour yellow, bronze and green leaves.

Beneath these is a row of petunias and below them are the brilliant yellow calceolarias. These are known as the slipper flower

A classic trough and hanging basket combination, with splashy colours and a wide variety of plants.

because of the intriguing shape of their pouch-like flowers. The hardiest varieties, suitable for outdoor use, include *C. mexicana*, which grows to 12 in (30cm) and produces ½ in (1cm) yellow flowers. Also recommended to me, though I have not tried them myself, are *C. chelidonioides* and 'Goldcrest', a dwarf perennial cultivar.

Then comes a row of magenta lobelia, an interesting alternative to more common blues, followed by a mass of trailing fuchsias. Along with pelargoniums and busy lizzies, fuchsias are the staples of summer window gardening. For all their delicate appearance they are hardy and bloom profusely throughout the summer to the last days of autumn. They can be used at the back of a box, to provide height; grown as standards, they makes superb feature plants for terrace tubs; and the trailing varieties are excellent at the front of a windowbox or in hanging baskets, as you can see here.

Though one sees lots of double-flowered cultivars on sale at nurseries, personally I find them a little too fussy. Fuchsias are elegant flowers with simple, distinctive shapes, and the doubles tend to look rather overblown. There are a superabundance of pinks and reds, but for something a little different look out for the trailing 'Thornley's Hardy', with small white and soft red flowers, 'Lady Thumb', a dwarf upright with red blooms and 'Hawkshead', with small white flowers and an upright habit.

All these fuchsias are the traditional rounded 'ballerina' shape, but I've noticed that varieties with long, tubular flowers are becoming increasingly popular. They tend to be rather plainer than the more common varieties but come in strong scarlets and orangey-reds that really command attention. Look for 'Thalia' and 'Jeane', which has small red and violet flowers and bushy pale green foliage. If I've spotted a fashion trend I shall be most pleased, because these are truly delightful plants.

Whichever variety of fuschia you choose,

your plants will be tolerant of a good range of conditions. In my experience they grow equally well on both south and north-facing windowsills, and though they require regular watering to keep them in flower they also cope with dry conditions for short periods. At the end of the summer remove the plants from the box, trim them back and put them in a frost-free spot over winter. Start water-

Hidden among these pots and troughs is an automatic watering system. The owner's favourite plants are the large daisy-flowered Dimorphotheca aurantica.

ing them again in spring, cut them back hard, and they will come to life for another year of splendid flowers.

A ROOF GARDEN WITH BEGONIAS

Sydney Arrobus's roof garden isn't very large, but it's crammed with beautiful displays of summer plants, most of them grown in windowboxes and troughs – an oasis of colour at tree-top level. Mr Arrobus has been a painter all his life and these days specializes in scenes painted around his home 'village',

Hampstead. As he's in his eighties, he's assisted by professional gardener Geoffrey Kaye, a mine of valuable information. He also has a computerized watering system, which waters all his plants twice a day. A few years ago, when he was using a less sophisticated type of device, there was a breakdown and both the terrace and the flat beneath it were flooded and needed major repairs. The latest system has an automatic cut-out facility to ensure that the water is turned off it there's a failure – something to bear in mind for anyone planning to install a watering system on a roof area.

There seems to be almost nothing Mr Arrobus doesn't grow in a container. There are trees, shrubs and climbers which include the grape vine in the background of this picture. You may also be able to spot sweet peas climbing through the vine, and a climbing geranium. The foreground trough contains a marvellous mound of *Felicia amelloides* and to the left is a pot full of brilliant phlox. Behind it is another box full of *Begonia semperflorens*, or fibrous begonias as they're better known. These plants have dark coppery-coloured leaves, a strong contrast with all the greenery around them. Other varieties have shiny green leaves and a wide selection of flower colour – everything from pale pink and white through to golden yellows and zinging reds.

Begonia × tuberhybrida grows larger than *B. semperflorens* and can be a useful way of achieving height in a box. Some of these plants have spectacularly large double blooms. For something that will really attract attention try 'Double Marbled Mixed', which has large double flowers speckled and marbled with white. Also available are trailing begonias which will drape spectacularly over the side of a container. Both types of begonia thrive in moist but well-drained compost in light shade. *B. semperflorens* is best treated as an annual, though if you pot it at the end of the season it will make an attractive houseplant. *B. × tuberhybrida* is grown from

tubers which can be lifted at the end of the season when the foliage withers. Dry the corms and store them over winter in boxes of dry peat for planting again in spring.

Other summer-flowering plants that can be grown from bulbs or corms include the low-growing cultivars of *Lilium speciosum*, with lovely trumpet-shaped flowers, and small-flowered gladioli. Depending on variety these can grow to around 2 ft (60cm) so put them at the back of the box. These tall plants are ideal if you're looking for privacy, not so good if you want to see out of the window. Also worth considering are elegant and unusual *Haemanthus multiflorus*, which produces large, red spherical flowers only six weeks after planting, *Allium karataviense*, which grows 6 in (15cm) tall and has pale pink flowers and large leaves, and *A. oreophilum*, with darker pink flowers.

For later in the year, at that awkward time when the annuals are over but it's not yet time for cyclamen or Christmas cherries for winter, grow autumn crocuses or colchicums. *Crocus speciosum* comes in delicate shades of blue, while the large corms of colchicums will produce flowers in abundance. 'Waterlily' is a particularly impressive variety, with double pink flowers. *Sternbergia lutea* looks very similar to a crocus and has bright yellow flowers. Just poke the bulbs into place 2 in (5 cm) beneath the surface of the soil in mid or late summer, and by mid-autumn you'll have new plants to take over from the tired summer annuals.

A COUNTRY HAY-RACK PLANTING

This planting is growing in a hay-rack style container that's been attached directly to the wall. I've included it not just because it's so attractive, but because it has been well

Windowboxes might have looked out of place against this old stone wall, but the hay-rack style planter is perfectly in keeping with the architecture.

COUNTRY STYLE

planted. There's not a glimpse of rack or compost in sight, just a deep, seamless spread of flowers and foliage.

As with hanging baskets, the trough should be lined first with a layer of sphagnum moss and then with a layer of plastic, which helps to retain moisture. The moss looks good even when the rack is first planted and there are gaps showing. Use heavy-duty plastic bin-liners and cut and tape them into shape, leaving the liner with a 'collar' slightly taller than the rack. Make plenty of small holes for drainage and fill with compost. The open top of the rack is easily planted and many people seem content to leave it as that and avoid the trickier and most important bit – planting the front.

Using a sharp trowel or scissors, cut small holes in the plastic at irregular intervals. Shake off as much of the soil as possible from the plant, trying not to do too much damage to its roots, and insert it into the holes. Make extra holes and fill in any obvious gaps and finish off by neatly tucking in any of the excess plastic at the top of the rack. When you first plant up this kind of container there will, of course, be quite a few small areas of

moss on show, but these should rapidly disappear as the plants grow. If there are any casualties later in the season they can be pulled out and replaced.

This particular hay-rack has been planted with an attractive combination of old favourites, including lobelia, verbena, helichrysum, trailing pelargoniums and fuchsias, and very good it looks. It will be more difficult to keep it looking good in the winter, and the main challenge at that time of year is to keep the lining covered. Ivy is probably the best way of coping. Plant two or three mature specimens along the top and, if necessary, another tier at a lower level. Top the lot off with a collection of brightly-coloured pansies, followed in spring by daffodils, tulips or polyanthus, and it will look a splendid sight all year round.

A PERENNIALS BOX

If you don't like the idea of a windowbox permanently planted with evergreens and don't want to replace seasonal displays three or four times a year, you might consider using perennials. These will continue flowering year after year and do not need to be

1 *Astrantia major*
2 *Anthemis cupaniana*
3 Trailing verbena
4 Osteospermum

An unusual box planted with summer perennials usually found in the herbaceous border.

removed from the box. The picture opposite shows a box planted up with summer perennials. At the back, its tall white flowers giving height to the scheme, is *Astrantia major* which begins flowering in early summer and will, if dead-headed and cared for, continue into early autumn.

Also in this box, though over when we photographed it, is *Alchemilla mollis*, commonly known as Lady's Mantle. This produces sprays of yellow-green flowers which seem to complement almost everything in the garden and are very useful for flower arrangers. The large pink daisy flowers are *Osteospermum*, sometimes known as Livingstone's daisy. Also in there are heartsease, *Viola tricolor*, and bold colour is supplied by purple and pink verbenas.

Though it looks so agreeable now, once the summer is over this box won't look so impressive. All these plants will die back during the winter months and there will be nothing to look at until next summer. For the owner of this box it isn't a problem. The box will be removed from the window-ledge in autumn and replaced with another permanently planted with evergreens, dwarf conifers, bulbs and winter-flowering heathers. But for many people this won't be a practical proposition and so the windowbox will have to be planted with a variety of perennials designed to flower throughout the year.

For spring colour one could use any of the bulbs mentioned elsewhere in this book, and trailing rock plants such as aubrietas, arabis and perennial candytuft. Hostas will begin to come into their own in early summer and other perennials for the sunnier times of year include *Dianthus*, rock roses and many rock plants such as achilleas, *Campanula portenschlagiana* and saxifrages, or any of the perennials in the box shown here. In mild conditions pelargoniums and fuchsias, usually treated as annuals, will prove themselves to be perennials, so there's no need to go without traditional summer windowbox plants. Autumn is a more difficult prospect. If looked after well, many of the summer perennials will still be flowering until the first frosts, but after that one has to rely on winter-flowering heathers and the bright berries of evergreens for interest until spring.

The great problem one stumbles across when planning a perennnials box is that if one is to have colour throughout the year there will probably be only a couple of plants in bloom at any one time. And while they are flowering there will be others that have lost their leaves or are not looking at their best, so one never really gets the kind of splendid display that can be achieved by temporary seasonal planting.

Where perennials come in really useful, particularly the low-growing or trailing rock plants, is as companions to evergreens. A mat of purple aubrieta or mound of saxifrage, followed in the summer by orangey-pink rock roses spilling from the front of a very plain evergreen box really brightens things up. This is where perennials do have the edge on seasonal plantings and where they are most useful.

CASCADES AND CLIMBERS

A very good windowbox should include a trailing plant or two to grow down the front of the box. Likewise, all boxes need a few taller, upright plants at the back to give height and form. Most of us are happy to settle for a few trailing ivies and perhaps some conifers to establish these effects. But some of the most interesting and spectacular boxes around are those which make a major feature of the trailing and climbing nature of the plants.

This is an element of windowbox gardening that is ignored by too many gardeners – myself included. It's a great pity, because nothing could look more spectacular in the summer than a window framed with Morning Glory, or a great cascade of nasturtiums or ivy-leaved pelargoniums reaching almost to the ground. Climbers and trailers are useful for hiding ugly architectural features – broken windowsills, nasty railings, downpipes, dirty rendering or brickwork, for example – but they don't need to be useful to be justified. Their great advantage is that they enable the ambitious gardener to make a major statement by transforming the house or building in a dramatic way.

Climbers require a bit more work, certainly. If you want to grow a clematis or Black-eyed Susan you'll have to go to the trouble of putting up a wire or trellis for it to climb, but that seems a tiny outlay for the kind of results you can expect. I've been fascinated by the way in which some people manage to clothe their houses using plants – and I hope you will be, too.

A CURTAIN OF COLOUR

This spectacular curtain of trailing pelargoniums was encountered quite by chance in Cheltenham. From the far end of the street we spotted a brilliant pink haze that appeared to emanate from a balcony and, sensing something special, raced to see what it was. It turned out to be the best display of ivy-leaved geraniums I've seen all year. Whoever waters, feeds and generally cares for these plants must have the dedication of a hospital matron.

The plants are arranged in tiers. They were so profuse that it was difficult to make out exactly how they had been organized, but the top row were growing out of boxes and beneath them, suspended from the balcony, were hanging baskets. The effect from the front is of an absolutely seamless cascade of red and pink flowers, with not a box or basket in sight.

Perhaps my only criticism of the display would be those small patches of yellow *Calceolaria integrifolia* that intrude here and there. Maybe they were included to tie the

colour scheme in with the yellow front door which, sadly, doesn't go very well with the flowers. In these circumstances I think I'd forget the calceolaria and paint the front door another colour!

At one time I lived in St Tropez and one of the great joys of gardening there was being able to take the shears and prune back the geraniums. They were so abundant that one had to work hard to keep them under control. Marguerites, too, grew in such profusion that if one wasn't careful they turned into hedges! This type of gardening was quite foreign to me as an Englishman; I was more used to have to encourage things to grow than cutting them back.

Even in England, though, a good spring and summer can bring a good flush of flowers from your ivy-leaved geraniums, followed by a hiatus while the plants recover themselves. That's the time to trim them back. It's hard when they've put on such growth but it's the best way of ensuring a strong second wave of blooms. When they have finished flowering in the autumn you can trim them back to about half their size and leave them in the windowboxes if you really want to, though their dry stems are really not a pretty sight during the gloomier months of the year. If you can, remove them, cut them back, put them into pots, store them in a frost-free place and forget them until the following spring – there's no need to water them.

AN UNUSUAL TERRACE PLANTING

When I started looking for examples of windowboxes for this book one of my aims was to find some slightly unusual plants, and this box contains two that are seldom seen. The first of them is a particular favourite of mine, *Thunbergia alata*, commonly known as Black-eyed Susan. One has only to see these

A splendid cascade of scarlet and pink trailing pelargoniums reaches down towards the smaller row beneath.

striking golden-orange flowers with their distinctive dark brown centres to know how the name originated. They are excellent trailers and climbers and need little encouragement to fall gracefully from a hanging basket or grow up a wire or string – or the railings of a roof terrace, in this case. If they are well cared for they can make an impressive 3 or even 4 ft (1m) cone of lush foliage and golden flowers that will continue in bloom until early autumn.

The reason we see so few of these attractive plants is that they are tender and require a sheltered, sunny spot to do well. In Britain they are recommended only for southern and south-western areas where the climate is mild. A second variety called 'Susie' has paler yellow flowers and is slightly hardier; it's seen here being grown as a trailer and will, given time, cover the guttering over which it is growing. A third variety, T. fragrans 'Angel Wings', has white flowers and is lightly scented. The first frosts of the year will finish all these plants but they can be grown from seed each spring and, if you have the right spot for them, make an unusual alternative to more traditional trailers and climbers.

Even more unusual are the two climbers which have been planted to grow up and along the railings. These are Eccremocarpus scaber, perennial evergreens in their native South America but in Britain more likely to be cut down by the first severe frosts. Their position on this terrace is probably too exposed for them to do really well, but if they are planted against a sheltered sunny wall these plants, known as Chilean glory flowers, can reach 10 ft (3 m) or more in a season. Their speed of growth is very useful for

Bright reds, golds and yellows soften the lines of a stark roof terrace. Just two months later the Black-eyed Susans had formed tall columns of leaves and flowers and the railings had virtually disappeared from view.

covering an unsightly wall or fence quickly. Perennial climbers such as honeysuckle, ivy or even passionflower will take two seasons to achieve what this plant manages in one. The orange, dusky pink and yellow tubular flowers gradually give way to extraordinary hanging seed pods which look intriguing in their own right and will supply a huge quantity of seeds for next year's plants.

These two climbers, Black-eyed Susan and Chilean glory flower, are particularly suitable for windowboxes. A south or west-facing window-ledge should offer the kind of warm, sheltered enviroment that both require, and because they have to be replaced each year there are none of the problems associated with growing a perennial climber. Other annual climbers ideal for training around the window include the cup and saucer plant, *Cobaea scandens*, which can grow to around 15 ft (5 m) in a season and from late summer to the first frosts carries distinctive purple or deep blue flowers shaped, as the name suggests, like a cup and saucer. 'Alba' has white flowers and in the right sunny, sheltered position can be even more vigorous. Another windowbox climber is the purple bell vine, botanical name *Rhodochiton atrosanguineum*, a delicate-looking climber which produces attractive pink and purple bell-like flowers until the first frosts.

One of the reasons so few of these plants are seen is, I suspect, because they are rarely available from nurseries and therefore have to be sown from seed each year. This requires a certain amount of planning and organization, but the results are well worthwhile. Once you have started the young plants and they're ready to go into the containers, one at each end, it's a very simple matter to pop a nail or two into the brickwork at each side of the box and tie a string or wire in place – no need for a trellis unless you really want to put one up. In a few months, when the window is surrounded by a profusion of attractive and unusual flowers, you'll be pleased you made the effort.

A BLAZE OF ORANGE

If you thought that single-colour plantings were boring, take a good look at this cascade of orange flowers. It shows what can be done on an ordinary windowsill simply by choosing plants whose heights and growing habits work well together.

At the back, a good 18 in (45 cm) tall, are two massive trailing-flowered begonias. The owner says that she knew they were going to be good plants when the first shoots began to appear just a few days after she'd planted the corms.

In front of these grows a row of bronzey French marigolds (*Tagetes*). There's something rather garish and flashy about them on their own, but used here as the middle link between the tall begonias and the trailers they give just the right intensity of colour and tight form. I always enjoy collecting plants and seeds and on one occasion when I was in Amman in Jordon I was shown over the royal stables by Princess Alia, King Hussein's daughter. There were wonderful marigolds everywhere, some of them just going over, so I collected the seeds and brought them home. It's always rather fun and evocative to bung them into an English garden and see what comes up – and when they do come up they bring back memories. It so happens that I'm on the council of St John of Jerusalem, which runs an ophthalmic hospital in Jerusalem, and I was asked to speak at one of their lunches. Queen Noor of Jordon was also there, so I was able to go to lunch wearing in my buttonhole a marigold from seed taken from their stables, which I thought was a rather pleasing touch.

Marigolds aside, at the front of the box, completing the cascade effect, are a dozen or so nasturtiums (*Tropaeolum majus*) in a range of colours from yellow, through orange to a deep red. Nasturtiums are attractive plants capable, with a little help, of climbing as well as trailing, and we would see many more of them but for one major drawback – they are quite irresistible to blackfly. This rules them out as far as many gardeners are concerned, and certainly none of the professionals I spoke to would even consider including them in a planting.

There is very little one can do to deter blackfly except to spray them regularly with a chemical mix containing pyrethrum or permethrin, a relatively new addition to the market.

The options for organic gardeners – and thank God everyone is trying to be a little

---

Begonias, marigolds and nasturtiums make a vivid colour combination.

1 Tuberous begonias
2 French marigolds
3 Nasturtiums
4 Helichrysum

more green these days — are less reliable. Prevention is better than cure, so try spraying with a mixture of washing-up liquid and water if the infestation is not severe, or a solution made of pulverized basil leaves steeped in water — said to repel most insects. The surest way is to remove the blackfly daily by hand, which is quite practical if the plants have been only lightly attacked but a serious undertaking if the underside of each leaf is thick with the pests, in which case it's best to snap off the affected leaves.

Theoretically this particular planting should not have worked. The nasturtiums require well-drained, poor soil and full sun to do well — a good choice if you tend to forget to water your boxes from time to time. The begonias prefer moist soil and light shade. The marigolds, fortunately, are tolerant of a wide variety of conditions. To improve the chances of all three species surviving together, the owner dug plenty of sand into the front of the box where the nasturtiums were to be planted and always watered into the back in the hope that the begonias would take up most of the moisture. These tactics are worth bearing in mind if you have set your heart on a planting that includes incompatible species. By adding extra peat to the compost surrounding a moisture-loving plant and sand or gravel around one that likes sharp drainage, you can get away with the most unlikely combinations.

AN ARCHWAY OF MORNING GLORY

This is a really effective way of using Morning Glory, one of the best annual climbers for windowboxes and containers. Two low troughs have been placed on each side of the steps leading to the front door of this house and from among the bedding plants emerge two blue-flowered Morning Glories, winding

This frightfully agreeable idea could be copied using other climbers, not just the Morning glory shown here.

their way up strings that are attached centrally above the doorway. It's not unusual to see these plants trailing over an arbour or trellis in a country style garden, but at the front door of a house in Chelsea it is a particularly pleasing sight.

The most common variety of Morning Glory is *Ipomoea tricolor*, which has large trumpet-shaped flowers in a clear shade of lavender-blue and is viewed by some people fortunate enough to have them growing wild in the garden as a weed. The white variety *I. alba* is also well-known. But you don't have to limit yourself to blue and white. Morning Glories come in a great variety of shades, from pink to scarlet and azure to indigo. For something really bright try 'Scarlet Star' with its red flowers each with a large white star radiating from the centre to give a striped effect. *I.* 'Platycodon Picotee' offers red and purple flowers with wavy white edges, certain to be admired. Most unusual of all is *I. imperialis* 'Chocolate', which has large flowers in a very subtle pinky-chocolate colour. Companion plants would have to be chosen carefully so as not to clash or detract from it, but it would make a very striking background to white or pale pink flowers or to a box planted with evergreens.

All these plants will reach 8 ft (2.5 m) or more and are easily grown up a string or twined through a trellis or the branches of an existing shrub. Once established they grow extremely rapidly and give extraordinary value for very little effort. They're ideal for framing a window, trailing over a porch or hiding an ugly architectural detail. I've also seen them used in hanging baskets, though they are so rampant that one would need to keep a constant check on them.

True to their name, Morning Glories are at their best in the morning and by later in the day their flowers will begin to fade. They should be planted in a south or south-west facing spot where they will get the light they need, though in a very hot summer they will flourish even in an easterly situation.

A TRANSFORMATION WITH IVY

This is a fine example of a house utterly transformed by the addition of windowboxes. In this case the boxes have been placed on the ground along the front wall and each contains a large-leaved variegated ivy (*Hedera colchica*). These have successfully covered large areas of the house and transformed the agreeable but rather stark frontage into something that is alive with colour and movement – a breath of fresh air in a street without front gardens or other greenery. Notice how the boxes are almost invisible against the background colour of the house so that the ivies make an uninterrupted statement. One other advantage has come of this planting, and that's the way in which the attention of passers-by is caught by the ivy and lured away from the windows, giving the house's occupants a little more privacy than they might otherwise have had.

It would be just as easy to grow these plants from a box on a windowsill. Given a little support they will swarm around a window, disguising unattractive walls, covering undesirable architectural features and softening any hard lines. Being evergreen they give year-round colour and cover. Unchecked they can reach a good 30 ft (10 m) in height but it is easy to prune them back whenever they become too much of a good thing. Once they are established they merely require watering, an occasional spray with a foliar feed and, annually, a pruning to remove any old, woody growth.

If you want to cover a smaller area then there is a wider variety of ivies to choose from. One of the most cheerful is the brightly variegated *Hedera helix* 'Goldheart', which has small leaves splashed with yellow and

Large-leaved ivies growing from ground-level windowboxes give a country air to this house, even though it's just a stone's throw from Park Lane in London.

gives tight, close cover. It climbs to around 6 ft (2 m) and would look particularly good if planted in a container with daffodils, yellow polyanthus or other yellow-toned spring bulbs. For extra colour in the summer it would be any easy matter to plant annual flowering climbers such as Morning Glory (see page 62) or *Eccremocarpus scaber* both of which would twine through the ivy.

If you don't like ivy there are other perennial climbers that will grow well in large windowboxes. The smaller, compact varieties of clematis, for example. Try *C. macropetala*, which has purple-blue flowers in late spring and early summer and looks just as good trailing abundantly out of a box to the ground as it does climbing a trellis, or *C.* 'Pink Champagne', a new variety. Clematis hate getting their roots hot, so don't plant them in plastic containers which hold heat in, or in a sunny position. Put evergreens or bedding round the base to provide shade. They require moisture but also good drainage, especially in the winter. Honeysuckles (*Lonicera*) may also be grown successfully in this way for two or three years, but the container has to be a good size. An acquaintance of mine bought a house which came complete with a Japanese honeysuckle in a window-box. It eventually had to be transplanted because, though beautiful, it required watering five times a day in hot weather.

The green leaves of Virginia creeper (*Parthenocissus quinquefolia*) turn a dramatic flame colour in the autumn, a splendid sight. It climbs by means of suckers on its tendrils and therefore requires no support, a very useful habit for those who want to cover a large area. The Russian vine (usually sold as *Polygonum baldschuanicum* but more correctly named *Bilderdykia baldschuanica*) is a real 'triffid' of a plant – so vigorous that if not kept in check it will take over anything and everything in its path. Not for nothing has it been nick-named the mile-a-minute plant. As well as moving quickly it can also reach 60 ft

(20 m) so needs to be used with care and cut back drastically. In the summer it is quite pleasing, with an abundance of foliage and long sprays of white and pale pink flowers.

Of course, all the plants mentioned above lose their foliage in the autumn and until the following spring one is left with more-or-less bare stems. These needn't look unattractive if the windowbox is planted up with winter plants and spring bulbs to distract the attention, but if you prefer foliage throughout the year it's advisable to stick to an evergreen climber – and ivy is, without doubt, the best and most reliable available.

A BOOZER'S BOXES – THE PROFESSIONALLY PLANTED PUB

The boozer of the title is my local pub, the Scarsdale Tavern, situated in South Edwardes Square just a short walk away from my home. The Scarsdale is the winner of a great number of competitions run by the Bloomin' Good Pub Award, London in Bloom and the Brighter Kensington and Chelsea Garden Scheme.

The front of the building is lost under a tumbling mass of ivy, fuchsias, trailing geraniums, lobelia, busy lizzies and a number of other varieties. This jungly effect isn't difficult to recreate. Boxes along the upper windowsills pour ivy and other trailers down into hanging baskets and the lower windowboxes. The overall impression is of one huge cascade of plants, with the large-leaved ivies (see page 22 for more on these) providing the main link between all the containers. Everything seems to thrive despite the fact that the site is overshadowed by a massive tree that cuts out a good deal of the light.

Perhaps the most striking touch of all are the huge *Fatsia japonica* in the window-

Beneath this jungle-like greenery is the Scarsdale Tavern, my local pub and probably the most lavishly planted public house in London.

boxes. These are already four years old and, according to Mr Weller who is responsible for the planting at the Scarsdale, have another four years to go before it's time to remove them. Despite their exotic looks, these plants are semi-hardy and survive without problems in a sheltered spot such as this. They certainly add an unusual touch to the traditional annuals.

Even in the hottest weather — and when we took the photograph the temperature was in the 90°sF (lower 30°sC) these boxes and baskets are watered only twice a week. The secret lies in the special compost, a combination of a number 3 potting compost (John Innes is probably the best-known) and houseplant mix, that Mr Weller uses. This, he assured us, holds water so well that you don't have to douse your plants every day. He also admitted breaking one of the cardinal rules of windowbox gardening; he doesn't feed his plants. I suspect that this is

Trailing ivies and pelargoniums make this lavish selection of plants a blaze of colour which virtually covers the building behind.

because his magic compost mixture includes a high content of slow-release fertilizer that will sustain the plants throughout the season.

The plants at this pub will be changed three or four times a year, depending on the weather conditions. For summer there is always a display of fuchsias, begonias, ivy-leaved geraniums and busy lizzies, all of them tried and trusted favourites. Petunias, marguerites and nasturtiums are never included, petunias because they tend to look untidy, even though they give a good, massy effect; marguerites because they are too much trouble, requiring almost daily dead-heading; and nasturiums because of their appeal to blackfly.

When these annuals are over in the autumn they will be replaced by cyclamen and heather. These will be succeeded after winter by daffodils and assorted bulbs. For the short but difficult period at the end of spring, when frosts are still a threat to summer annuals, bright blue and pink cinerarias will be added to ensure that there's never a day when the Scarsdale doesn't look a delight — and the bitter's good too!

PROBLEM PLACES

Many of the windowboxes discussed in the previous pages are pretty tolerant and will flourish in a wide variety of situations, but what can you do if your window-ledge is subject to particularly difficult conditions? Shade is a problem in cities, where tall buildings cut out the light and cast great shadows. Sun can also be a killer if you live high up in a south-west facing flat where there is no shade at all. The only solution is to choose plants whose growing habits are best adapted to these situations. For a parched window-ledge, look for natives of Australia or South Africa, which will be used to heat and sun. For a gloomy, overcast spot choose plants that are normally found in shaded woodland situations and will actually flourish in the semi-darkness.

Looking around for windowboxes suitable for difficult conditions, I was surprised at how attractive and well-planned many of them were. It's as if a problem situation focuses the mind. With a limited number of plants to choose from, gardeners seem to come up with particularly agreeable ways of beating the problem.

A PLANTING FOR A
SHADY POSITION

Shade can be a major problem for the town gardener. It's not so much a matter of aspect – even a north-facing ledge normally gets enough light to grow most plants – but of shadows cast by tall buildings nearby, or gloomy basements which see the sun for only an hour or two a day. Faced with this kind of problem many windowbox gardeners give up when their pelargoniums and lobelia fail to thrive, or their bulbs grow leggy and unattractive. Which is a pity because, as you can see from this box, it's possible to grow a good display in adverse conditions.

This box was brought into the sun for the photo, but it normally occupies a north-facing windowsill which gets little light because of a large tree nearby. The owner, having tried and failed with ordinary bedding plants, did some research and came up with this attractive combination in a stylish green and white colourway. The plants which immediately catch the eye are the hostas, *H. fortunei* 'Aureomarginata' and the smaller *H.* 'Thomas Hogg' (an ideal hosta for container planting), with their bold, sculptural shapes and foliage edged in cream. They are a good choice, appreciating shaded, moist conditions. Another attractive variety is *H. fortunei* 'Albopicta', whose leaves are yellow-green in spring, gradually turning to patterns of two-tone green. Hostas produce pale mauve flowers on a 2 ft (60 cm) tall stem in mid-summer, but these are of secondary importance.

In autumn the hostas and the busy lizzies

This elegant green and white planting will survive in the kind of shady conditions that are death to sun-loving plants.

PROBLEM PLACES

will fade and the owner plans to replace them with *Asplenium trichomanes* (maidenhair spleenwort), which has curving evergreen fronds. These grow well in pots and so could be plunged into the gaps left when the busy lizzies are removed.

In the centre of the box is planted an *Alhyrium felix-femina* 'Minor' and crisp white busy lizzies (*Impatiens* 'Ancient White'). Busy lizzies like a semi-shaded spot but, in my experience, are tolerant of a wide variety of conditions. They are really good value for money, flowering from mid-spring through to mid-autumn if they are well fed and properly watered.

Other plants that will do well in shade include azaleas and rhododendrons and camellias, all of which are evergreen and will provide interest throughout the year. Creeping fig (*Ficus pumila*) is evergreen and although sold as a houseplant, will flourish on a protected windowsill out of the sun. Its neat oval leaves, black stems and trailing habit makes it a good alternative to ivy. Kept moist, it should survive a mild winter unscathed. Creeping Jenny (*Lysimachia nummularia*) is also evergreen, has soft, green, small, rounded leaves and quickly forms a trailing curtain several feet (metres) long. Its small, butter-yellow flowers may not be to everyone's taste but in the cultivar 'Aureum' they are far less significant against the gold-green leaves. They are easy-going and will flourish in either sun or shade as long as conditions are moist.

A PLANTING FOR A
SUNNY POSITION

Most gardeners tend to view shade as more of a problem than sun, but an exposed south-west facing windowsill which gets full sun for a large part of the day can cause its

A box for a hot spot; the exotic-looking yucca and calocephalus brownii will take all the sun they can get.

WONDERFUL WINDOWBOXES

own set of difficulties – particularly during the kind of summer we enjoyed in Britain in 1989. The problem is compounded if you are unable to water the plants at least once a day.

This box has been planted with hot, sunny conditions in mind and the result is a rather exotic, Mediterranean look. At the centre is a yucca, which will survive throughout the year in a sheltered spot. Planted around it are brilliant pink trailing *Verbena* 'Sissinghurst', a plant which thrives in full sunlight and gives an excellent display of colour throughout the summer. In the past I have found them difficult to come by, but it has been good to see them in more common use in the last couple of years. Among the verbenas is *Dorotheanthus bellidiformis*, commonly sold as mesembryanthemum and known as the Livingstone daisy. This plant comes from South Africa and is, as you might imagine, well-adapted to hot, dry conditions. It comes in a variety of colours, from strong orange and bright red to more subtle shades of pink and yellow, and in our northern climate gives a wonderful show from early summer into the early autumn as long as temperatures are not too high.

Helichrysum petiolatum is used for its trailing quality to cover the front of the box, but *Calocephalus brownii* is the real show-stealer. A perennial silver plant from Australia, it has curly, wire-like stems covered in small leaves. Easily cultivated from cuttings, it thrives in hot sun. Also in this windowbox is *Sedum spurium* 'Tricolor', its variegated foliage tinged with pink flowers into the autumn.

Other suitable windowbox plants that can cope with full sun and very well-drained (too often a gardener's euphemism for 'dry') soil include *Portulaca grandiflora*, commonly known as the sun plant, which has masses of

brilliant purple, red or yellow flowers that open in sunlight. Try also the Star of the Veldt (*Dimorphotheca aurantiaca*), another South African plant and in some ways a larger version of the Livingstone daisy, with brilliantly coloured flowers in red, strong orange, salmon pink, pale yellow and white. Also from South Africa come gazanias, large daisy-type flowers in shades of yellow and white that rise from broad mats of foliage. Still with a daisy-style flower is *Layia elegans*, popularly known as 'Tidy tips' because each golden petal has a white tip to it. Marigolds, particularly 'pot marigolds', so-called because in medieval times they were used for cooking, can take tough conditions as long as they are regularly dead-headed, as can many forms of *Dianthus*. Nasturtiums, too, do best in dry, sunny positions. For flowers from late winter to early summer try *Arabis caucasica* 'Variegata' which grows in low, spreading mounds and positively thrives on dry soil and sun.

THE CHEAT'S ALTERNATIVE

If your windowboxes are in a difficult position, or if you're simply too busy to look after them yourself, there's only one acceptable way of cheating – and that's to get someone else to plant and maintain them for you. It's an alternative I've had to resort to myself in recent years because of the amount of time I spend abroad, and I've found it to be remarkably successful and surprisingly reasonable. A professional windowbox company will plant your boxes seasonally so they always look attractive, water them weekly, and generally maintain and care for them. I really can't recommend this service too highly. Local newspapers and telephone directories will supply details of companies offering this kind of service in your area. Some garden centres will make up custom-planted windowboxes and containers to suit your requirements, though you will still have to water and look after the plants particularly in hot and dry weather.

This eye-catching arrangement of plants is a novel arrangement making optimum use of the space.

THE EDIBLE
WINDOWBOX

The idea of home-grown fruit and vegetables appeals to many people, particularly in view of current concern over the pesticides and chemicals that seem to be sprayed on practically everything we buy. Windowbox gardeners can't expect to grow-their-own in a serious way, but it's possible to produce small amounts of fruit, vegetables and herbs on your windowsill. And even if you only end up with enough strawberries for a garnish, or enough tomatoes for half-a-dozen salads, there's still something rather rewarding about having grown them yourself.

Miniature vegetables seem to be all the rage at the moment which is good news for anyone gardening on a limited scale. Small is beautiful; cherry tomatoes, carrots only a couple of inches (centimetres) long, cauliflowers and lettuces no larger than a tennis ball, tiny but sweet Alpine strawberries — they're all rather special and they're all perfect for growing in a windowbox. So are herbs, and because one often doesn't need more than a couple of leaves at a time from a plant, it's a very practical and economical way of growing them.

Fruit and vegetables are easy to grow and require no more time or effort than flowering plants. They will, though, need daily watering and regular feeding, which will make them inconvenient for some people. Almost everything you could wish to eat can be grown from seed, but as such small quantities are required to fill a windowbox or two, it's simpler to buy your strawberry, tomato and herb plants from a nursery and get your box off to a flying start.

Of course, you don't have to give over a whole windowbox to growing edible plants, though many of them have good flowers — chives, thyme, sage and strawberries being examples. But if you don't want a box given over completely to fruit and vegetables it's very easy to grow a few lettuces, a tomato plant, some parsley or a row of radishes among the summer annuals so that you get the best of both worlds; beautiful flowers *and* a quick nibble at the same time.

A PLANTING WITH
ALPINE STRAWBERRIES

Alpine strawberries are tiny but deliciously sweet, ideal for windowboxes because of their delicate foliage and neat growing habit.

You won't obtain a great deal of fruit from these few alpine strawberry plants but the berries have the intensely sweet and true flavour of freshly cultivated/real strawberries. Add them to fruit salads or use as a garnish.

THE EDIBLE WINDOWBOX

An added bonus is their mouth-watering strawberry scent. They may be grown easily from seed – from sowing to the first crop takes only three months – or can be bought as young plants from most nurseries. In the spring they have pretty white flowers which make them attractive plants in their own right. They require plenty of water and regular feeding, but if treated well will reward you with fruit from early summer right through to autumn.

There are several varieties of Alpine strawberry; those shown here are an old variety, 'Baron Solemacher'. For something rather different try 'Alpine Yellow' which is, true to its name, a golden colour and is reported to have a wonderfully intense flavour. This variety is particularly useful if you have problems with birds; apparently yellow strawberries are not as attractive to them as the traditional red ones.

Trailing from the front of the box is *Lysimachia nummularia* 'Aurea'; behind the strawberries are feverfew (*Chrysanthemum parthenium*) and marguerites, their white flowers echoing the strawberry flowers.

A wide variety of other vegetables and fruits can be grown in windowboxes. Sweet peppers should grow well on a sheltered south-facing windowsill in the south of England. You will probably have to sow them from seed, in which case look out for Thompson & Morgan's 'Canape F1 Hybrid', a pepper designed for cooler northern climates. Aubergines can also be grown successfully this way.

Flower-petal salads were all the rage four hundred years ago and seem to be rather fashionable again. You can grow your own in a windowbox, starting with lettuce (see below for suggestions) and interplanting with nasturtiums, borage, mint, marigolds and violas. Carefully pick off a selection of

These may not be the prettiest windowboxes in the world but they're a vegetarian's delight.

fresh flowers, wash and toss with the lettuce. Your dinner guests will be appalled!

If you'd like something a bit more substantial than strawberries or flowers on your plate, you could try growing mini-cauliflowers. Seeds can be sown directly into the soil and the cauliflowers are harvested when they are about 3 in (7 cm) in diameter – the perfect size for one person. Sown in early spring among the summer bedding plants, the cauliflowers should be ready to pick by early autumn. More spectacular still are ornamental cabbages. These extraordinarily eye-catching vegetables come in green-and-cream and green-and-red varieties, with wonderful veined and variegated effects, some of them with frilly edges to the leaves. The leaves only begin to colour when the temperature drops to below 50° F (10° C) so these are ideal plants for late autumn and winter. And when you've had enough of them in your windowboxes they can be cut and eaten or used in indoor flower arrangements, where they'll look even better than they do on the windowsill.

TWO BOXES
PLANTED WITH VEGETABLES

No one can pretend that windowboxes planted with vegetables are the prettiest of sights. No matter how much care is taken with them, the plants simply don't grow in as orderly a way as more traditional windowbox plants – but that is their charm. If you're bored with pelargoniums and busy lizzies and want to grow something that will be useful, then think fruit and vegetables.

I once saw a house where the owners had planted a living curtain of runner beans up and over a side window which was too easily overlooked from the pavement. And there's a place in Sussex where in the summer tufts of carrot foliage mingle with the bedding plants in the windowboxes. Neither of these two windowboxes can rival those, but each has a lot to offer.

The rear box is planted with cherry tomatoes, in this case 'Gardener's Delight', though 'Sweet 100' and 'Red Alert' are also recommended. These grow well in windowboxes, especially plastic ones which retain the moisture the tomatoes require. As the tomato plants grow, pinch out some of the side trusses and generally guide the plant into an attractive shape. Apart from this they require regular watering and feeding with a liquid fertilizer – special tomato fertilizers should be available from all garden supply shops. By spraying the plants when they are in flower you can help them to 'set', i.e. to produce fruit. Growing among the tomatoes are marigolds and basil, traditional companion plants. The marigolds are said to repel whitefly, while the pungent aroma of basil seems to deter a variety of insects. My wife uses chopped basil leaves to make a delicious accompaniment to a tomato salad! The nasturtium flowers, visible at the front of the box, can also be eaten in salads but they were planted for another purpose – luring backfly away from the other plants.

It was so hot on the day we took this picture that the lettuces in the front box wilted the moment we put them in the sun. They are green 'Salad Bowl' and a red variety, 'Red Sails'. Both are cut-and-come-again lettuces which will go on supplying salad leaves throughout the summer. 'Red Sails' turns a deep bronze when the temperature drops to 80°F (26°C) or below, but because of the very high temperatures at the time we took the picture it had lost its dramatic colour.

Fortunately the other contents of the box weren't so badly affected. At each end is an unusual purple dwarf bean, 'Blue Coco', which has attractive mauve flowers and eye-catchingly dark, almost black, pods. Certainly rather different – and absolutely delicious. The centre of the box contains small globe-shaped 'Parmex' carrots. Unless you have exceptionally deep windowboxes, choose a similarly small variety such as 'Suko' which grows to only 2½ in (6 cm) in length and, as miniature vegetables are very much in fashion at the moment, is considered rather smart. The remaining space in the box has been planted with parsley (good as a garnish with the carrots and beans) and nasturtiums which are doing an excellent job as decoys, attracting the attention of the blackfly from the beans. Like the tomato box, this one also requires plenty of water and regular doses of liquid fertilizer to ensure a decent crop.

The only limitation when it comes to growing vegetables in windowboxes is size – but that still leaves plenty of scope. Try a combination of radishes and spring onions among the bedding plants; dwarf *mange-tout* peas; mixed lettuces; sweet peppers; fennel; new potatoes; even baby beetroot, which will provide attractive red-veined foliage.

A HERB BOX

For the enthusiastic cook, what could be better than a box filled with herbs, like this one planted by the Marshalswick Horticultural Society which I saw at the 1989 Chelsea Flower show? It is packed with useful herbs, including parsley, purple-flowered chives, variegated mint, a tiny borage plant with its blue flowers just beginning to show, sweet bay rising in the centre of the box, violas and nasturtiums (whose flowers can be added to salads) and thyme. At the sides rise the ferny foliage of fennel and tucked into the gaps are red oak-leaf lettuces.

Other good culinary herbs include rosemary for use with lamb and chicken, basil for use with tomatoes and sweet basil for use on pizzas and in soups and stews, marjoram, sage and coriander for Indian or Greek dishes. Many of these herbs can be picked and dried for use throughout the year.

Fresh herbs for the kitchen windowsill.
Leaves can also be dried in the microwave for seasoning all year round.

SOMETHING DIFFERENT

Looking around for windowboxes to photograph and write about in this book I came across a few that were a bit different from the rest. These were all boxes planted with a theme or a philosophy in mind. There's a Chinese-inspired landscape created as an aid to meditation, a buttonhole box which was the result of a whim, and more ideas to inspire you to indulge your own whims. All of them have an original creative spark, even though they're not, perhaps, the kind of thing I would choose for my own windowsill. What they've shown is that the only real limit of windowbox gardening is imagination. Why not put the pelargoniums and busy lizzies aside for a while and let your imagination rip? The result may be a surprise – and a delight.

A BUTTONHOLE PLANTING

When I first started thinking about this book I decided it would be fun to include a few slightly curious windowboxes that could be given as presents or planted up with special interests in mind. How jolly it would be, I suggested to the publishers, if we included a 'buttonhole' box with carnations, for the person who likes a fresh buttonhole every day. Well, here, after some considerable experimentation, is the result, photographed in the conservatory.

The gardener who planted the box decided to combine the carnations with ferns and hit upon this combination of 'indoor' ferns and *Dianthus chinensis*, commonly known as the Indian pink. As you can see, it looks rather splendid. *D. chinensis* was chosen because it is more tolerant than ordinary pinks and can cope with the moist soil and light shade necessary for the ferns.

The ferns used in the box are all commonly available. They included small *Nephrolepis exaltata* 'Bostoniensis', more commonly known as the Boston fern, the Cretan brake fern (*Pteris cretica*) and a number of wispy emerald ferns, sometimes erroneously known as asparagus ferns because of their Latin name, *Asparagus densiflorus* 'Sprengeri'. This latter trailing fern likes a position with cool, filtered sun, which makes it ideal for planting at the front of the windowbox where it will receive more light.

This combination of ferns and pinks lived happily on an exterior north-facing windowsill for some time during the very hot summer of 1989. The ferns benefited from being planted in a terracotta pot because the water evaporated from it quickly and created the kind of humid environment they require. This in turn has a pay-off for the *Dianthus*, which were not left sitting in waterlogged compost as they might have been had a plastic

container been used. When eventually the *Dianthus* began to show signs of needing more light, they were removed, potted up and plunged in the garden. While they were recuperating in the main bed, their place was taken by a couple of fuchsias which were better suited to the conditions. I don't suppose anyone in their right mind would actually wear a buttonhole including a sprig of Boston fern (I certainly wouldn't!), but the result of the experiment is an agreeable sight.

The advantage of a small, attractive windowbox planted like this is that it can serve as both an outdoor and an indoor box. These ferns and a wide variety of other plants normally thought of as houseplants are quite capable of surviving outdoors in a sheltered spot during a warm summer. As autumn approaches one has only to tidy up the evergreens, remove the annuals and add seasonal flowering or foliage plants and one has an attractive box for the conservatory.

A SCENTED PLANTING

The importance of scent came home to me when my eighty-year-old mother took up with a toy-boy in his seventies, who had just gone blind. He was an artist and had painted all his life and for someone who had so appreciated the beauty of things, to go blind at seventy was quite dreadful. Scented flowers were quite wonderful for him and I'm sure that a scented windowbox would be appreciated by anyone whose sight is impaired.

On an irrelevant but rather amusing note, my mother and her toy-boy always used to worship together in Chester where they live,

These lush green ferns will live outside in the summer and can be brought back into the conservatory as the temperature drops. The Dianthus *prefer more light and less water, so should be considered as a purely temporary addition.*

and on one particular Sunday they decided that instead of going to their usual church they would go to the cathedral. So off they went, and when they got there they found the place was full. Down the aisle there were men wearing medal ribbons and carrying flags, which mystified my mother. Eventually the verger came forward and asked if he would help them. 'I'm not really quite sure where to sit', said my mother.

'Who are you?' asked the verger.

'General public,' muttered Douglas, her toy-boy.

'Oh, do come this way,' said the verger, and escorted General and Mrs Public down the aisle and sat them next to the Lord Mayor. My mother, of course, could see what was happening and was horrified, but Douglas had no idea at all. It turned out that they'd unknowingly gate-crashed the annual

1 Lily
2 Dwarf stock
3 Tobacco plants
4 Lavender
5 Scented-leaved geranium
6 Dianthus
7 Pineapple mint
8 Pink alyssum
9 Thyme

This scented box would make a perfect present for someone whose sight is impaired.

service for the Cheshire Regiment. After the ordeal my mother telephoned me, deeply mortified, and told me what had happened.

'It's a good job you didn't say "Private citizen",' I told her, 'or you'd have had to sit at the back.'

Anyway, back to scented plants. The owner of this box had never tried a scented planting before and wanted to use as many different plants as possible to see which performed best. At the back of the box are some dwarf stocks, grown from seed and transplanted from the garden when they were about 9 in (22 cm) high. They are flanked by mixed tobacco plants, *Nicotiana alata*. Those with white and lime-green flowers are the most scented – some of the reds and pinks have no perfume at all. The pink lily, probably a *L. speciosum* cultivar, was bought, unidentified, as a houseplant, but its heavy, sweet scent is overpowering in all but the largest rooms. In a windowbox, however, it is ideal; it is also surprisingly hardy and is resistant to most diseases. It will definitely be included in next year's planting.

Another great success were the two clumps of *Dianthus* – one pink and the other pale golden yellow. Both flowered profusely throughout the summer and into autumn, providing not just a good scent but also flowers for cutting. The yellow miniature rose was not such a success and will be transplanted to the garden at the end of the season. Its space will probably be taken by another scented-leaved geranium like the two in the current box. Their pink flowers, variegated leaves and delicate lemony perfume are a pleasure. You can take cuttings from them in the autumn for next spring, or over-winter the plants indoors.

Also in this box, though over when we came to photograph it, is *Lavandula angustifolia* 'Hidcote', a dwarf lavender with purple-blue flowers. This, like the rose, will be transferred to the garden at the end of the season. Though pretty, it does not contribute as much interest or perfume to the box as

anticipated. At the front of the planting are a number of scented trailing plants including a pink *Alyssum*, probably 'Rosie O'Day', and a thyme in full flower. Even more useful for its scent is the lemon-scented thyme, *Thymus × citriodorus*, whose leaves are strongly aromatic.

The bushy mint at the front of the box is pineapple mint which, according to the owner, smells lovely but not at all of pineapple. Mint is easy to grow – so easy, in fact, that given time the pineapple mint will take the box over. Plant it in its pot, which helps to contain growth.

Scented annuals that the owner could try out next year include Sweet William (*Dianthus barbatus*), some varieties of purple petunia, which have a strong scent in the evenings, dramatic Cherry Pie (*Heliotropium × hybridum*) with its dark green leaves, purple flowers and scent of almonds, wallflowers (*Cheiranthus*) and even dwarf sweet peas such as 'Snoopea' and 'Cupid', which could look attractive tumbling down at the front of the box. One final suggestion for those people, like the owner of this box, who love cats. Why not grow *Nepeta × faassenii*, more commonly known as catmint, for your pet? As well as driving cats wild it has an aromatic scent and provides spires of lavender-coloured flowers from early summer right through to the autumn.

A DRIED-FLOWER WINDOWBOX

For those gloomy interior windowsills where not even the toughest houseplant can survive, the only option is to forget plants altogether or to fake it.

This windowbox arrangement was made by an acquaintance of mine, Simon Lycett. The container is a hand-made terracotta trough – bought, I shall reveal, at a discount

Dried flowers make a very agreeable permanent display in a variety of positions in the home.

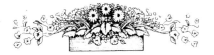

because the bottom was slightly cracked. This made it unsuitable for exterior use but perfectly fine for use indoors. There's no need, of course, to choose a real windowbox like this. Any container that fits the window-sill will do. Fill it with crumpled chicken wire, as here, or with tightly-packed blocks of dry foam into which dried roses, oats, nigella, orange-tufted carthamus, spiky green and purple-brown amaranthus and dahlias have been inserted.

There's a huge variety of dried flowers available for arrangements to suit all kinds of interiors and colour schemes. Garden centres selling dried flowers and specialist suppliers of both finished arrangements and loose flowers can be found in most areas. If you have a garden of your own you might care to use your roses, larkspur, peonies, delphiniums, gypsophila, *Alchemilla mollis* and Chinese Lanterns – just a few of the many common British varieties suitable for drying. If you live in Australia or South Africa then the exotic shapes of the banksias and proteas will be available to you. Pick the flowers when they first begin to bloom and hang them upside down in a warm, dark place to dry. This can take a couple of days or several weeks, depending on the plant. When they are completely dry they are ready to be used. When you come to arrange them, roses and peonies look better if they are gently steamed over a kettle for a few seconds and then opened out.

Of all the windowboxes in this book, this is the one that requires least maintenance and lasts longest. Careful dusting is all that is required to keep it looking good. Dried flowers do, however, fade. They are, therefore, strictly for the gloomiest windowsills – those in basements or at the side of a house, where the sun never shines.

This miniature landscape is intended to aid meditation and create a sense of calm and well-being.

A CONTEMPLATIVE WINDOWBOX

This Chinese-inspired trough was planted by Suchin Ee, one of Britain's leading exponents of *penjing*, a style of gardening that pre-dates bonsai. In the Chinese Sung dynasty poets and scholars were sent from the city to the mountains, which were considered to be the oldest natural phenomena. There they meditated, contemplated and were inspired by the natural beauty around them. When they returned to the Emperor's court they told of the tranquillity they had found and of the life-enhancing effect of the mountains. The Emperor ordered the recreation of the mountains in miniature, so that he could enjoy them himself. Courtyards were filled with small-scale representations of the mountains, and to make them more realistic tiny trees, whose roots were pruned to prevent them from growing, were added. Thus were the arts of *penjing* and bonsai begun.

Suchin Ee, a regular exhibitor at Royal Horticultural Society shows, continues the *penjing* tradition. Her troughs are works of art in themselves, sculptures made of chicken wire covered in cement and then coated with peat, gravel, marble chippings, dust and anything else she can find. Each trough and the rocks in and around it are different. Trees are planted in shallow dips filled with soil. The tall tree at the front of this trough, with two trunks, is *Sagaretia theezans;* the others are *Chamaecyparis* of various sizes. All have been taken from cuttings. The other clumps of greenery are moss, scraped from garden walls and paths and placed on a thin layer of mud over the concrete.

Running water plays an important part in *penjing* because its soothing sound aids meditation. One doesn't have to be a Buddhist to appreciate the effect. The waterfall in this trough is powered by an electric motor hidden under one of the rocks – which can be removed if anything goes wrong. The piping is also hidden. The finished result is a

WONDERFUL WINDOWBOXES

1 Tradescantia
2 Ornamental cabbage
3 Red herringbone or prayer plant
4 Spider plant
5 Nidularium
6 Croton
7 Dracaena 'Red Edge'

A box filled with indoor plants chosen for the colour and shape of their foliage is a good way of brightening an interior windowsill.

miniature landscape, the rocks symbolizing permanence, the water the impermanence of life.

This kind of trough will flourish on a wide, sheltered window-ledge or balcony and would be particularly appropriate in town. Its attractions are quite different from those we normally appreciate in windowboxes; no riotous colours or rampant growth, just stillness, stylized form and tranquillity in the middle of all the noise and activity of city life.

AN INTERIOR WINDOWBOX
Windowboxes don't have to be used exclusively to brighten up the exterior of a house. If you have a convenient interior windowsill there's no reason why you can't have an

indoor windowbox. Containers packed with houseplants are nothing new, of course, but in my experience they never seem to last very long. Flowering plants are over quickly, trailing plants get straggly, and too often one finds a thirsty plant sitting alongside one which can survive for a month without water. A well-planted interior windowbox like a good exterior one, should last for months without the need for constant supervision.

For professional advice we consulted a company specializing in interior plant displays. They explained that their policy is to use only plants that enjoy the kind of conditions they are likely to experience in homes and offices – and that includes central heating, responsible for the deaths of so many houseplants. Watering is simplified by using troughs with no drainage holes in the bottom. Drainage is supplied by a 2 in (5 cm) thick layer of expanded clay pellets at the bottom of the box, covered in some cases with a layer of capillary matting which draws up water from the reservoir created by the pellets. The plants are removed from their pots and placed directly onto the matting so that their roots can obtain the moisture they require, and the gaps between plants are filled with soil. Once the trough has been thoroughly watered it should be able to go a week, or perhaps a month, without watering.

For best results, don't use flowering plants in an indoor trough. Flowering plants require dead-heading and, once their season is over, don't make much of a contribution to the display. It's better to concentrate on plants with interesting and colourful foliage. As you can see from this example, the result can be most agreeable.

At the front of the box the boldly-marked leaves of the prayer plant or red herringbone plant are flanked by two cabbages which command immediate attention. These will probably need to be removed and replaced after a couple of months, but make an excellent feature meanwhile. A large spider plant, creeping fig (*Ficus pumila*) and tradescantias trail over the front of the box, concealing the plastic. At the back are a variety of plants with interesting leaf and colour detail. They include a *Nidularium sp.* with pink-tinged, razor-edged leaves; a croton, whose bright red, yellow and green-patterned leaves add a good splash of colour; a *Dracaena* 'Kiwi' and another *Dracaena* which is usually known sold as 'Red Edge'; a *Dieffenbachia sp.*, more commonly known as a dumb cane; and an arrowhead plant (*Syngonium podophyllum*). These plants all enjoy the kind of warm conditions they will be subjected to in this centrally-heated kitchen. If you have a particularly sunny windowsill fill the back of the box, which will get most sun, with plants that flourish in heat and light. Plants low down at the front of the box will get less light because of the shadows cast by those behind them, so look for something, like the creeping fig and prayer plant, that can cope with a shadier position.

HANGING BASKETS

Not every house has window-ledges or space for windowboxes, and not every householder wants to go to the trouble of planting and maintaining troughs throughout the year, but that doesn't mean one has to forget gardening altogether. Hanging baskets are the ideal way of creating a bright splash of colour throughout the summer, and when it's over they can be taken in and stored until the following year. There need be no worries about autumn, winter or spring plantings – unless, of course, you want to create a year-round display.

Used in combination with windowboxes, a hanging basket or two at the sides or over the top of a window can complete the whole effect. See how well they work in the picture taken in Stratford-upon-Avon on (page 100) or at the Scarsdale pub (page 68). Hanging baskets look fine used singly at the side of a front door, but for the most spectacular displays you'll need several of them. Hung together from a wall, half-a-dozen will be enough to stop people in their tracks.

PLANTING UP

The best hanging baskets are simple wire ones with large gaps to allow plants to be inserted at the sides. Avoid the solid plastic pots in which trailing fuchsias and pelargoniums are often sold. Once they are hung up there's often more pot than plant on view. Line the wire basket with sphagnum moss and then with a layer of plastic, leaving a collar of plastic sticking up above the edge of the basket. Pierce the bottom and sides a few times for drainage and then fill with compost. Hanging baskets can dry out very quickly so choose a mixture specially formulated for containers and baskets or take a tip from Mr Weller who plants the boxes and baskets at the Scarsdale Tavern (featured on page 68) and make up a mixture of a number 3 potting compost and houseplant compost.

Start planting around the sides, using scissors or fingers to make a hole in the plastic and hollow out a space for the plant's roots. This can be a difficult process if the basket keeps tipping and moving, so find something on which it can be supported while you work. Try an upturned colander or bucket. When the sides are covered, fill the top and tuck any remaining plastic neatly away inside the basket. To finish, hang the basket up at a convenient height and add another plant or two – perhaps an ivy – at the bottom. When you've finished you should have a good ball shape and soon the whole basket will be covered in flowers and leaves.

BRACKETS AND SUPPORTS

Most garden shops offer a variety of hooks and brackets for supporting hanging baskets. The type you need will depend largely on the position you've chosen for the basket, but most people use some kind of right-angled bracket. Do try to find something that complements the style of your home. Many of those on sale are made of wrought iron,

which is functional but isn't quite right if you have a very formal home. If the garden centre doesn't have what you're looking for, try an ironmonger or D.I.Y. supplier who may have alternatives to offer. Some of the smartest hanging baskets I've seen were supported on very plain brass brackets to match the letterbox and doorknocker. Most of these hanging basket fixings can be put up with just a couple of holes and screws, a job that doesn't require any great D.I.Y. skills.

One last point, which seems very obvious but is often forgotten, is to hang the baskets somewhere they can be easily maintained. They may look terrific dangling 8 ft (2.5 m) off the ground but if you need a ladder to water them each day you'll end up wishing you'd been less ambitious. The opposite is also true; don't hang them so low that you're constantly banging your head on them! A number of gadgets for watering hanging baskets are on sale. Most of them involve a plastic container of water and a long tube with a downwards U-bend at the top. By pumping or squeezing one can send water up the tube and into the hanging basket. I've seen one of these being operated and it seemed pretty hard work, but something like this would be worth investigating if your hanging basket *has* to hang in a difficult spot.

PLANTS FOR HANGING BASKETS

Hanging baskets contain so little compost that they are very quickly dried out by the wind and sun. It's therefore important not only to water them regularly but to choose plants that can cope with occasional dry spells. Choose trailers or plants with a neat, mounded growing habit – nothing too tall or upright to stick out at an angle from the rounded shape of the basket. The old

Hanging baskets are used to a delightful effect on this lusciously planted house front. Emulate this, and you'll spend your whole time watering.

favourites are the best. Fuchsias and ivy-leaved pelargoniums are both very reliable and will give the basket plenty of volume. Fibrous and trailing begonias, busy lizzies, lobelia, campanula, petunias, *Helichrysum petiolatum*, nasturtiums, trailing verbenas, tradescantia, *Sphaeralcea munroana* (with greyish foliage and pinky-purple flowers), Creeping Jenny (*Lysimachia nummularia*), creeping fig (*Ficus pumila*) and Black-eyed Susan are all ideal. Remember to choose the right plants for the right aspect – pelargoniums, verbenas, and nasturtiums, for example, for a place in full sun, busy lizzies, mimulus and begonias in shadier spots.

Most hanging baskets are planted to create a riot of colour but if you would like a more formal effect they can look equally good in just one or two shades. I quite like single-colour plantings of busy lizzie in spherical wire containers. The finished effect is of a neat, tight ball. Pastel pink and apricot seem to be the favourite colours, but brilliant scarlet or cerise would look good against a white wall. Campanula, a plant with delicate-looking blue or white bell-shaped flowers, makes a fine display though its flowering season is shorter than many other species. A pink and grey basket planted with petunias, ivy-leaved geraniums, verbena, busy lizzies and plenty of grey-leaved *Helichrysum petiolatum* and *Senecio maritimus* would look wonderful, and for a really sizzling effect you could combine purple petunias and dark blue lobelia with deep pink pelargoniums and strong red busy lizzies.

A HANGING BASKET
AND MATCHING CONTAINER

The lovely lavender-blue flowers of *Felicia amelloides* make an eye-catching feature in this hanging basket. It's a good shape, finished by the trailers which cascade almost to the ground. Also included in the planting is mimulus, commonly known as the monkey flower, another good annual for window-boxes because of its strong colours and form. Mimulus flowers are wide trumpet shapes and come in a variety of colours including flaming scarlet, purple, orange and yellow, many with blotches of darker colour. They will bloom freely from mid-summer to mid-autumn, though like petunias they tend to become straggly as they get larger. Two strains ideal for hanging baskets in shady positions are 'Shade Loving Mixed' and 'Hybrid F1 Malibu', both producing compact and vigorous plants. Mimulus need moist soil and enjoy a shady site.

The container behind the hanging basket is planted with pink trailing pelargoniums and verbenas, petunias, lobelia, busy lizzies and fuchsias. A splendid way of cheering up a dull corner.

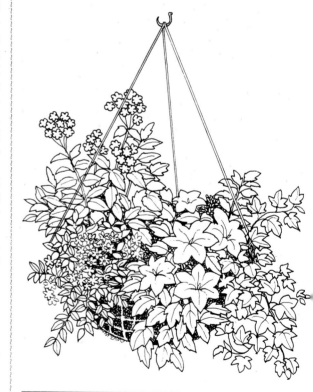

What better way to fill a picturesque corner than with brightly-coloured hanging baskets?

A ROW OF HANGING BASKETS

This row of six hanging baskets was photographed in Stratford-upon-Avon, where we had to join a queue of tourists waiting to take a picture! Each basket is slightly different from its neighbour which makes the finished effect that much more interesting. Among basic plants such as fuchsias and lobelia there are yellow calceolaria, blue and white campanula and multi-coloured petunias.

Variations on a theme – more hanging baskets.

HANGING BASKETS

FINISHING TOUCHES

I suppose if one wants to be pedantic, a book about windowboxes should contain nothing more than pictures of windowboxes on windowsills – in which case I have already erred by including hanging baskets and free-standing troughs in the previous pages. So I shall compound the error by squeezing in a brief chapter on other kinds of containers.

During my research for this book I came across not just wonderful windowboxes but many other container plantings, some of them providing additional touches of colour to houses where boxes and hanging baskets were also in bloom. Whether they were as cheerful as the rows of small pots overbrimming with lobelia and placed on each side of steps up to a front door, or as sophisticated as the elegant white tubs containing perfectly clipped cubes of box, all were features

that improved the look of their surroundings – which is why I've included them here. If windowboxes and hanging baskets seem too ambitious or time-consuming a prospect for you, try planting up a single tub. It will require very little maintenance and it will help to brighten our streets.

In theory it's difficult to imagine a more unlikely combination than this Egyptian-style statue and the terracotta pot with a euonymous and marguerites, both on the steps of an elegant London town house. But surprisingly they work together to make a most agreeable feature of this front garden. If you have a striking piece of statuary consider using it as part of the exterior decor of your home – it's likely to be too heavy for most passing burglars!

GETTING IT RIGHT

THE RIGHT WINDOWBOX

When we look at other people's successful windowboxes we tend to focus on the plants and flowers on display and ignore the containers in which they're growing. So it's easy to assume, when we come to planning and buying windowboxes of our own, that the boxes themselves are of minimal importance – which is a mistake.

Good windowboxes enhance the look of the buildings on which they are situated. They complement the shape, size, and structure of the window and suit the architecture. And they look good not just in the summer, when they are almost hidden by flowers, but in the winter and spring when they are most exposed.

Unfortunately, in the excitement of the first hot spell of the year and a hurried visit to the garden centre, this tends to be forgotten. The results can be awful. You've probably seen examples of this lack of planning yourself. A 2 ft (60 cm) long box sitting forlornly in the middle of a majestic 8 ft (2.5 m) windowsill; a bright orange terracotta pot clashing wildly with the red brickwork of the house; an ornate, embellished ironwork trough sitting proudly on the sill of a minimalist 1960s office building; or a plastic box streaked with green algae disgracing the front of a white stucco townhouse. Perhaps the saddest thing of all is that once the owners of such windowboxes realize they've made a fundamental mistake, they tend to lose interest in the whole project and the box

and plants rapidly become an eyesore. But just a few minutes' thought before setting off to buy boxes can make all the difference between success and disaster.

THE RIGHT SIZE

The best-looking windowboxes are those that neatly fill their sills. Large, well-fitting boxes are also more practical than small ones. The larger the box, the more plants you can use and the better the display. Larger boxes hold a greater volume of compost which means that they don't dry out as quickly as smaller boxes, so less watering is required. And, worth bearing in mind if your house abuts the pavement, a large, close-fitting box is less likely to be stolen from the windowsill than a smaller, free-standing and easily portable one.

But what if your windowsills aren't a standard size? Or if you've set your heart on some particularly beautiful boxes that don't fill your windowsill? There are several ways of solving the problem of an awkward shaped or sized window-ledge. The first is to make your own windowboxes, by no means the daunting prospect it sounds. Turn to page 111 for practical advice on making and maintaining your own containers. If do-it-

This bay window has custom-made windowboxes running right round the sill, with the result that the plants have become an integral part of the design of the house.

GETTING IT RIGHT

A simple home-made wooden fronted 'fake' windowbox.

yourself boxes are out of the question, any carpenter or joiner will be able to produce made-to-measure windowboxes quickly and cheaply. There are also many companies who specialize in supplying, planting and maintaining custom-made windowboxes, lifting the entire burden from your shoulders. Look in the telephone or local business directory for details.

A second solution is to give the appearance of a fitted windowbox by making a simple 'front' for your window-ledge, behind which you can hide a variety of different containers to make up the required length. I've seen this done very successfully using two lengths of softwood cut to the width and depth of the sill and nailed together to make an L shape – a kind of backless windowbox. Once painted or varnished this structure is placed on the windowsill and the containers put in position, where their weight holds everything in place. Additional fixings can be added to give extra stability.

This type of fake box has several points in its favour. It's cheap and can successfully disguise a motley collection of containers – the example I'm thinking of hid from view a

number of old tin cans and plastic pots which were being used to contain the plants. If you have a particularly long windowsill which would require a heavy and cumbersome single windowbox, it enables you to use a number of smaller, easier-to-handle containers while, from the front, maintaining the appearance of a single smart box.

Many very attractive windowboxes – terracotta and ceramic ones, in particular – come in small sizes because it is impractical to make them on a larger scale. These boxes are too good to hide behind a false front, but they often leave an unpleasingly large gap at each end of the window-ledge. If this is your problem consider filling the gaps with pots or small tubs made from the same material as the windowbox. Planted with evergreen shrubs (try azaleas or camellias), box trees or plants with an upright habit (for example, daffodils for the winter, lilies in the summer) these pots won't just look impressive; they'll also make the entire windowsill look as if it has been cleverly designed and co-ordinated. If you're using free-standing windowboxes you may need to use a driptray beneath them. On a low sill excess water draining

away doesn't cause problems, but if your window-ledge slopes backwards towards the wall or directly overhangs a street a driptray will prevent water damaging the wall or sill, and keeps people passing in the street beneath dry.

A final point to bear in mind when sizing up boxes is proportion. Many mass-produced containers are quite shallow and low, and on a large windowsill they can look lost and insubstantial. If you have a particularly wide or tall window, look for taller, deeper containers to match. Made to measure boxes, designed for a particular window, will always look better than mass-produced ones. As a general rule of thumb, the bigger and grander your windowsill, the bigger and grander should be your boxes and the display in them.

THE RIGHT MATERIAL

The most commonly available kind of windowboxes are made of plastic. I really don't like plastic boxes and would urge anyone thinking of buying them to investigate all the other options first. That said, they are cheap and strong and, if they're made of reasonably heavy-duty material, should last years. If your windowsills are unsound or you plan to stand your windowboxes on brackets, plastic is the best material; it is considerably lighter than the other options and so requires less support. Plastic boxes are ideal for growing vegetables and moisture-loving plants because, unlike terracotta for example, they retain water well. For this reason they are not the best choice for alpines, nasturtiums, clematis and other plants which like good

A backless windowbox held in place on a recessed window-ledge with fixings.

drainage and cool roots. The depressing drawback of plastic windowboxes is that they tend to look stark and mass-produced and they can be a real eyesore if left unplanted throughout the winter and spring. To counteract this, plant plenty of ivies and trailers so that the harsh lines of the box are covered throughout the year.

Wooden windowboxes, custom-made to fit individual ledges, are difficult to beat. They are inexpensive, particularly if you make your own, and look much better than their plastic counterparts even when they're not planted. The main drawback of wood is that it has to be painted or treated every year or two and, if not looked after, rots. But by using a wood preservative and supporting the box on blocks so that it isn't in direct contact with the sill, a timber container can last a long time. An additional bonus, especially for anyone living in an elegant town house, is that wooden boxes can be painted to match the rest of the exterior and hence unite the outside decoration.

Terracotta troughs are reasonably priced and can look charming, particularly when they have aged and lost some of their bright red colour – though new boxes can be toned down immediately by soaking them thoroughly and rubbing them with mud. Water evaporates from porous terracotta more quickly than from plastic or wood, which makes it ideal for plants that like dry conditions but unsuitable for those that like cool, damp soil. The main problem associated with this material is its fragility and tendency to frost damage. If you have terracotta pots that are not guaranteed frost-proof, bring them into the garden shed or conservatory during the winter – there's nothing more disheartening than a frost-damaged favourite.

Reconstituted stone or concrete troughs and boxes have an impressive appearance and come in a wide variety of shapes and designs. They are particularly good for free-standing displays along a low wall or on a terrace, where their weight can be well supported. Unless you have a really solid windowsill it's probably best to go for one of the other types of box – stone troughs are extremely heavy when they are empty; when full of wet compost they may be impossible to move. For this reason stone boxes are not the best choice for porch roofs or flat-roofed extensions, neither of which are strong, or for supporting on brackets. Their great advantage is that they age well and look wonderful when covered in moss and lichen. If you've set your heart on a stone trough but are worried about its weight, take a look at some of the plastic 'stone-effect' containers now on sale. They're much lighter and can be rubbed down with soil which helps to create an 'aged' effect. Once planted up with plenty of trailers it's difficult to distinguish them from the real thing.

Fibre-glass and lead both make good containers that wear well and require little maintenance. Lead is heavy; fibre-glass is light. The only real drawback is that both types of box are sometimes inordinately expensive your planting will have to be spectacular to match them.

Ceramic planters make useful indoor-outdoor containers. They are not frost-proof and so must be brought inside during the cold months. These planters are stylish enough for the conservatory or sitting-room during the winter and in the summer months they make good outdoor boxes. Many of these planters are imported from Spain and the Far East, and personally I think it's best to be wary of those with exotic or brightly-coloured patterns if you're going to put them outdoors. Blue dragons or brilliant Moroccan-inspired designs can look hideous on British windowsills.

Stone boxes can be dangerously heavy. Here a small one is used on the window-ledge while below an impressive free-standing trough offers a larger planting area. The pavement and the house are thus linked.

WONDERFUL WINDOWBOXES

THE RIGHT STYLE

Windowbox style is a matter of taste – and I won't hesitate to say that for town window-boxes my taste leans towards something simple and unobtrusive. My own window-boxes are made of black-painted wood and I chose them because they complement the style of the house and make a good back-ground for the plants inside them.

When buying boxes for your own window-sills, take into account the architectural features and the style of your home or office. You may fancy terracotta troughs, but how will they look against the grey pebble-dash of the house? In such a situation, classic white wood or white plastic might be the best compromise. On the other hand, if you live in an old cottage, plastic may look totally out of place. A word of warning about stone troughs. They come in a wide range of shades from pale cream, through honey-coloured Cotswold stone to a cool grey. Choose the shade that goes best with your house.

I'd advise strongly against boxes that are too fussy or ornate. A wrought-iron or rustic bark-covered box may be all right in the summer when it's overflowing with flowers, but how will it look in the winter? Is it honestly in character with your house and the rest of the street? Discretion is also required if you have a flat in a building where other residents have already established win-dowboxes. In this case, consider choosing something that will match the existing troughs and planting. It may not be entirely to your own taste but, viewed from outside, the building will look better if the boxes complement rather than fight each other.

THE RIGHT COLOUR

Plastic windowbox manufacturers offer their wares in a variety of greens and browns as well as white. Some people choose the green because they feel that it is the most 'natural' colour. Personally, I think this is usually a mistake, particularly in town. Manufacturers tend to go for sludgy, indeterminate greens that create instant dinginess and may even clash with the foliage of the plants. Beige, too, looks horrid unless the fabric or paint-work of the house matches or complements it. In a rustic setting these colours don't seem so bad, but to my eyes they look awful against the bricks and concrete of so many city homes. If you have to have a plastic box, white or the very dark green or brown ones that have appeared on the market in the last year or two look somehow less ghastly and more discreet than pea-green or beige.

Wooden boxes can be painted any colour you like, an advantage if you're keen on splashy pillar-box red or sunshine yellow containers or want to match them to the colour of the window-frames or front door – not that I like red or yellow front doors, personally. Plastic boxes are easily painted with spray car paint which comes in a wide range of colours, though depending on the type of plastic and weather conditions you may have to do a regular re-spray.

MAKING, PLANTING AND MAINTAINING YOUR WINDOWBOXES

D.I.Y. WINDOWBOXES

If you have a few basic D.I.Y. skills you'll find wooden windowboxes are easy to make; you certainly don't have to be a skilled carpenter to turn out something that will do both you and your window-ledge credit. Start by measuring up and working out what height, width and depth are going to look best for your window. Is the box going to stand on the sill or be supported by brackets? If the latter applies, your box can be deeper and wider than the window-ledge.

Most boxes are made of pine or other softwood, but if you fancy solid mahogany there's nothing to stop you using it except concern for the world's rainforests. Cut the wood to size and drill half-a-dozen drainage holes in the piece that will form the bottom of the box, then nail all five bits firmly together. If the box is going on a sill, make a couple of 'feet' from offcuts and attach them to the bottom so that water draining from the soil can escape. And there you have it, one custom-made windowbox.

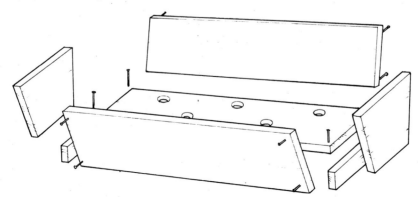

It is quite straightforward to make your own wooden windowbox. Drill large drainage holes and tack strips of wood under the base to raise it off the ledge.

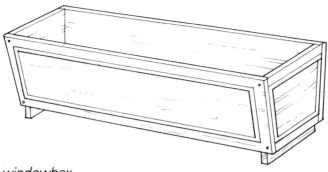

A simple wooden windowbox.

This basic box won't last long unless it's given some form of protection, so paint the interior with a couple of coats of wood preservative. Some preservatives are harmful to plants; look out for non-toxic brands at your local garden centre. The exterior can be rubbed down and painted or varnished to suit your taste. For a particularly impressive effect add beading to make a panel at the front. The paint finish is entirely a matter of your own choice, as simple or sophisticated as you care to make it. I've recently seen wooden boxes painted to look like marble or with painted ivy trailing down the front. Give a decoratively-painted box a coat or two of varnish to protect it. For a tough matt finish you could try using sandy-textured paint, the kind normally used on exterior walls.

FIXING THE BOXES

Boxes resting firmly on ground-floor window-ledges shouldn't need to be fixed into place unless you're worried about having them stolen. If security is your concern you can make them theft-proof by screwing an eye-hook into each end of the box and a corresponding one at each end of the window-frame. Put the box in position and connect the two eyes with strong wire.

Boxes on high ledges should always be secured as a matter of safety. Use the method described above or, if you want to take them down to replant them, use a hook and eye system. If the window-ledge is narrow and the box protrudes from it, it can be supported by brackets attached to the wall beneath the window, or by supports screwed into the sill beneath the box. These have short, upturned ends that prevent the container sliding from the ledge. If there's no windowsill at all, or if the window opens outwards and thus prevents you from having a box at sill height, use wall brackets to fix it

A hook and eye attachment will keep your windowbox in position.

wherever it's convenient. When choosing your brackets bear in mind not just the size of the box but also the weight they'll have to support. Most boxes require just a couple of brackets, but a really hefty container may require more.

Brackets are relatively easy to install. You'll need a masonry drill bit, the appropriate-sized rawplugs and screws and a spirit level, to make sure the brackets are all at the same height. If the idea of drilling holes and screwing in brackets while up a ladder is off-putting, it shouldn't cost the earth to get a builder or handyman to do the job.

If there is a very narrow ledge, fix your box to the wall with brackets.

With brackets you can fit your box to your chosen spot on the wall.

A free-standing box, ideal for a ground floor window.

COMPOSTS

The best windowbox and container composts are those you can buy commercially from garden centres. The big companies all produce mixtures specifically for this purpose. They are relatively light, peat-based composts with a good balance of nutrients. If you're worried about your boxes drying out or want to grow moisture-loving plants you could try a home-made combination of one of the standard No. 3 composts and houseplant compost. This is said to be particularly good for retaining water during the summer, though it may not be such a good idea in winter when plants may become waterlogged.

Peat-based composts should be replaced every 12-18 months. By that time most of the nutrients will have been used up and plants will not do so well. If you're planting your container permanently with evergreens and perennials, it's best to use a soil-based compost such as John Innes potting compost No. 3, which can go for three years or more without needing to be replaced. Alpines require a special, gritty soil.

Before you start filling your box, check that it has drainage holes. Many plastic boxes have their drainage holes marked but not drilled through. You'll have to do this yourself using a drill or, if the plastic is not too thick, a screwdriver. Allow two or three drainage holes for each foot (30cm) in length, more if the container is very wide or deep. Some terracotta, stone and ceramic pots have no drainage holes at all. If this is the case with yours, you'll need to fill the bottom with a couple of inches (centimetres) of broken crocks or stones from the garden. Don't use gravel for this level, it's too fine, but do use it for a further 2 in (5 cm) layer over the stones and crocks. Horticultural sand (not builders' sand) can be used if gravel isn't available.

If you have drainage holes in your container there's no need to bother with this, though a few broken crocks over the holes will ensure that they don't become clogged with compost. It's not a good idea to underestimate the importance of decent drainage. Waterlogging can be just as much a problem as drought.

WATERING

In an ideal world the compost in a windowbox would be slightly moist at all times. In practice, as windowbox gardeners know, this is impossible. A terracotta box on a sunny windowsill may well require watering twice a day, and between those two soakings it may become quite dry. A plastic box in a shady spot, however, may need watering only once a week, even in summer.

Deciding when your windowbox needs watering can be difficult. Poking a finger into the compost isn't so easy when the entire box is covered with foliage. And anyway, though the top inch (centimetre) may seem quite dry, beneath the surface the soil may still be wet. If you're uncertain of whether the box needs a good watering or not, fill it to the rim and see what happens. If the water is very quickly absorbed and nothing drains away at the bottom, do it again. Leave the box for a few minutes before testing with your finger. If the top layer is still damp, that's probably enough water, but if it has already dried out you should add more. In the winter windowboxes require very little water at all; be careful not to drown them.

An easier solution is to use a water-meter. These are usually marketed for use with

---

The same idea for boring steps as on page 120 but a totally different result! These steps have been lined with pots that overflow with lobelia, blue and pink petunias, busy lizzies and pink and white pelargoniums. The blues make a vivid contrast to the bright red front door and are echoed in the bold purple and white petunias and dark lobelia in the windowbox. Hooray for red, white and blue.

houseplants, but a horticulturist acquaint-ance of mine swears by them for all kinds of containers. One simply sticks the prong of the meter into the soil and it immediately registers the moisture content. By inserting the prong at different depths you can dis-cover whether your windowbox is waterlog-ged at the bottom and dry at the top, or parched throughout. One of these water-meters would make the ideal gift for a friend with a window garden.

In summer water your windowboxes when they are out of direct sunlight, preferably early in the morning or in the late evening when temperatures are low. You can avoid scorched leaves and flowers by taking the sprinkler off the watering can and watering directly into the compost so that the plants themselves don't get wet.

The principles mentioned here also apply to hanging baskets and all other types of container. Hanging baskets, being complete-ly exposed to the elements, may require watering several times a day in a heatwave, so keep a regular check on them. It is also wise to mist plants over during dry spells, though not when they are in direct sunlight.

FEEDING

For a really good display of summer annuals in a windowbox you will need to apply a liquid feed every ten days. Though the compost will supply the nutrients they need to get started in the first few weeks of growth, these fairly soon get exhausted. It's wise to begin feeding a month after planting and to keep it up throughout the summer. There's a huge variety of fertilizers on the market, some of them claiming to have been specially formulated for windowboxes and containers. They may well be very good, but any fertilizer with a good potash content will suffice to produce plenty of flowers. Any of the several available liquid tomato fertilizers, all high in potash, will work well. If you're keen on organic gardening look out for seaweed-based organic fertilizers.

ROUTINE MAINTENANCE

Apart from watering and feeding, the most important thing you can do to encourage your plants to put on a brilliant display of flowers is to dead-head them regularly. With some plants, mostly those with lots of small flowers, it's an almost daily job. Others may require dead-heading only once a week. Dead-heading doesn't just keep the window-box looking neat and tidy but, by preventing the development of seeds, it actually encour-ages more flowers to be formed.

Many plants that flower and then seem to fade can be encouraged to flower again if you trim them back. Ivy-leaved geraniums often become straggly and cease flowering after a first flush in early summer. Cut them back by about a third and, if you're feeding and watering them properly, they should put on another spurt. Windowboxes look at their best when they're abundant, not when they're out of control. If your plants are getting too big and losing their shape, or if their growth is getting straggly, don't hesi-tate to keep them in check by trimming them back.

PESTS AND PROBLEMS

Even the best gardeners find their plants occasionally blighted by pests and diseases. These are the most common problems likely to be encountered in windowbox gardening.

Aphids – also known as greenflies and blackflies. Aphids suck the plant's sap, weakening it and causing yellowing leaves and distorted growth. Busy lizzies, cyclamen, roses and nasturtiums are prone to the problem. The organic solution is to pick the aphids off by hand. Non-organic gardeners should spray the plant with an insecticide containing permethrin or pyrethrum.

Black stem rot – pelargoniums are particularly susceptible to this problem. It starts at the point where the stem enters the potting mixture but soon spreads upwards with stems becoming blackened and spongy. This problem occurs when compost is too wet over a long period. There is no cure, but cuttings can still be taken from healthy tops of affected stems.

Leaf miners – leaf miner grubs tunnel between the surfaces of leaves, leaving behind them a criss-cross pattern of white lines. Marguerites and cinerarias are particularly susceptible. Treat the problem by picking off the affected leaves and applying the appropriate insecticide.

Mildew – makes its appearance as powdery grey or white patches. It is usually caused by overwatering and humidity (sometimes as a result of too many plants packed together densely in a container, with little air circulating). Begonias are among the worst sufferers. To treat, pick off the affected leaves and spray the rest of the plant with the appropriate fungicide.

Red spider mites – these tiny insects suck sap. The leaves turn mottled and unattractive and may eventually fall off. As red spider mites like dry, hot conditions it's sometimes enough to mist the plants regularly so that their dampness repels the pests. Otherwise use an insecticide.

117

Slugs and snails – these common pests can decimate a windowbox by eating the stems and leaves of any juicy plants. They come out mainly at night, hiding among the foliage in the day. Pick them off the plants whenever they appear and inspect the bottom layers of foliage every few days. If necessary sprinkle the compost with slug pellets, but do this only as a last resort; poisoned slugs may be eaten by hedgehogs, who will in turn be poisoned.

Of course, it's not just pests and diseases which can disrupt plant growth. If your plants begin to look unhappy but there is no sign of infestation or disease it may be that their growing conditions are unsuitable. Use this check-list of symptoms to help diagnose the problem.

Spindly growth, with pale leaves and large gaps between them; small or unexpectedly few flowers; plain leaves instead of the expected variegations. The problem in this case is likely to be lack of light. Move the container to a position where it will receive more sun and the plants should show improvement.

Wilting leaves and stems; yellow or brown patches on the leaves; stunted growth. Plants suffering from these symptoms are probably receiving too much direct sunlight. They'll do better in a shadier spot.

Yellow-toned leaves; leaves dropping off. These symptoms are caused by overwatering. Remove yellowed leaves and cut back on water.

PLANT LISTS

Unless specified, plants are suitable for most ordinary situations and soils.

EVERGREEN SHRUBS AND PLANTS

Many of these shrubs grow to several feet (over a metre) in height and will need to be pruned if they are to remain a suitable size for windowboxes. Buy young plants and look for dwarf varieties. Move those that eventually outgrow the windowbox to the garden.

Asplenium scolopendrium and varieties: 'hart's-tongue fern'. Damp shade.

Azalea: dwarf varieties suitable. Bright spring/early summer flowers. Plant in lime-free compost. Shade.

Buxus: 'Common box'. Useful for clipping and formal shapes. Slow-growing.

Camellia: choose small varieties for large troughs. Flowers late winter/early spring. Plant in lime-free compost. Shade.

Chamaecyparis lawsoniana cultivars: conifers. Variety of shapes, colours and sizes.

Cotoneaster dammeri and *C. microphyllus*: low-growing, draping habit. Orange-red berries, white flowers in early summer.

Erica carnea: winter-flowering heather. Variety of colours.

Euonymus fortunei: silver and gold-variegated forms.

Hebe: dwarf varieties suitable. Foliage varies from dark green to silver-green and grey-blue. Spikes of purple or white flowers in autumn.

Hedera species and varieties: ivies. Trailing and climbing varieties, wide range of leaf shapes, sizes and variegation.

Juniperus communis: smallest conifer, 2ft (60cm) tall. Spire shape.

Laurus nobilis: 'bay'. Clip to make formal trees.

Pieris formosa var. 'Forrestii': new spring leaves are scarlet, then cream, finally turning green for winter.

Rhododendron: dwarf varieties suitable. Plant in lime-free compost. Shade.

Skimmia japonica: shiny green leaves, red berries, white flowers.

Variegated japonica: shiny green leaves with yellow variegations. Red berries, white flowers.

SUMMER ANNUALS

As well as true annuals this list includes other plants that are best treated as annuals. Unless specified, they are suitable for most ordinary conditions.

Alyssum maritimum: 'sweet alyssum'. Scented. White or lilac flowers, bushy or trailing 3–6in (8–15cm).

Antirrhinum: 'snapdragon'. Variety of bright colours. Look for smaller varieties 6–12in (15–30cm).

Begonia semperflorens: fibrous-rooted begonia. Bushy plants with bronze and green foliage, red, pink, or white flowers 6–12in (15–30cm).

Begonia × tuberhybrida: tuberous begonia. Bushy and trailing varieties in broad range of colours up to 18in (45cm).

PLANT LISTS

Calceolaria: pouch-shaped flowers in yellow, red and orange 6–12in (15–30cm).

Campanula: trailing bell-shaped flowers in blue or white 6–8in (15–20cm).

Coleus: foliage plant with leaves variegated in bright shades of red, pink, green, cream, purple and yellow 12–18in (30–45cm).

Dahlia: choose dwarf bedding varieties 12–20in (30–50cm).

Dianthus: 'pinks'. Wide variety of cultivars with pink, red, white and apricot flowers. Scented, 6–12in (15–30cm).

Dimorphotheca aurantiaca: 'Star of the Veldt'. Large daisy-type flowers in yellow, orange, pink and white. Sun.

Felicia amelloides and *F.bergeriana*: blue marguerite-style flowers, fern-like foliage, up to 18in (45cm) and 4–6in (10–15cm) respectively.

Fuchsia: trailing and bushy varieties, with pink, red, white, purple and scarlet flowers. Height varies – it's possible to have standard plants 3ft (90cm) tall – but normally 1–2ft (30–60cm).

Helichrysum petiolatum: silver-grey trailer, felt-like leaves. Also lime-green cultivar.

Hosta: perennial foliage plant with broad green leaves, some edged with cream or variegated. Damp shade required.

Impatiens: 'busy lizzie'. Perennial, usually treated as annual. Wide range of colours, including pink, red, white, mauve and apricot 6–12in (15–30cm). Shade.

Lobelia erinus: low-growing and trailing. Dark and light blue, white, magenta, pink and violet. 4–6in (10–15cm).

Matthiola incana: 'stock'. Choose dwarf varieties. Scented. White, mauve, pink, red. 12–20in (30–40cm).

Mesembryanthemum criniflorum: 'Livingstone daisy'. Bright pink, yellow, orange and red daisies. Trailing. 4–6in (10–15cm). Full sun.

Mimulus: 'monkey flower'. Red, orange and yellow flowers with purple, yellow and cream blotches. 8–12in (20–30cm). Moist conditions.

Nemesia strumosa: small, funnel-shaped flowers in red, yellow, pink and blue. 8–10in (20–25cm). Moist conditions.

Nicotiana alata: 'tobacco plant'. Star-shaped flowers on tube-like stems. Scented. White, lime green, pink, cream and dark red cultivars. 1–2ft (30–60cm).

Pelargonium: geranium. Trailing ivy-leaved varieties have smooth, shiny leaves and white, pink, red, maroon and lavender flowers. They trail 3ft (90cm) or more. Upright zonal cultivars come in a similar range of colours, some with variegated leaves. Size varies greatly but is usually in the 12–18in (30–45cm) range. There are also scented-leaved varieties.

Petunia: large funnel-shaped flowers in white, pink, mauve, red, purple. Star-patterned and white-edged flowers also available. 8–12in (20–30cm). Sun.

Phlox drummondii: look for dwarf cultivars. Bright red, mauve, pink and white clusters of flowers. 10–12in (25–30cm).

Portulaca grandiflora: 'sun plant'. A trailing mat of bright purple, yellow or red flowers. 6–10in (15–25cm). Full sun, dry soil.

Pyrethrum ptarmaciflorum: lacy-leaved bushy silver plant. 12–16in (30–40cm).

Salvia splendens: bright red spikes of flowers above bright green leaves. 12–16in (30–40cm).

Senecio maritimus: hairy silver-grey leaves, delicately intersected for a lacy effect. Look for dwarf varieties 18–24in (45–60cm).

Tagetes erecta: 'African marigold'. Look for

What to do with boring steps: Without these attractive pots this corner would look rather bleak. Here steps get a pastel treatment with a series of terracotta pots full of conifers, pink busy lizzies and pelargoniums. Half the pleasure of the arrangement is that the pots complement each other without matching. A matched set would look too contrived. These, each with a different plant, keep the eye busy.

small cultivars. Clear yellow and orange 12–24in (30–60cm).

Tagetes patula: 'French marigold'. Look for small varieties. Domed, full flowers in yellow, orange and bronze. 8–12in (20–30cm).

Tropaeolum majus: 'nasturtium'. Trailing orange, yellow and red flowers on long stems with broad green leaves. Full sun.

Verbena: trailing and bushy varieties. Clusters of tiny flowers with dark green leaves. Colours include purple, pink, white and crimson. 6–12in (15–30cm).

Viola: 'pansy'. Choose summer-flowering varieties, large or small flowers in a range of colours including yellow, white and blue. 6–10in (15–25cm).

Zebrina pendula: 'wandering Jew'. Trailer with green and cream striped leaves.

Zinnia: mop-headed flowers in bright pink, orange, yellow, scarlet, crimson and purple. Choose smaller cultivars. 8–16in (20–40cm).

CLIMBERS

Clematis: perennial. Look for smaller cultivars, particularly those recommended for use in containers (e.g. *C. macropetala*). Early and late-flowering varieties in a range of colours from white and pink through to violet-blue. Climbs to 3–4 yards (metres) up wires or trellis.

Cobaea scandens: 'cup and saucer plant'. Annual. Purple or white cup-shaped flowers from mid-summer to first frosts. Climbs to 4 yards (metres) up wires or trellis. Requires a sheltered spot.

Eccremocarpus scaber: 'Chilean glory flower'. Treat as annual. Orange, salmon and pink trumpet-shaped flowers. Climbs to 3 yards (metres) up sticks, wires or trellis.

Hedera: wide variety of evergreen climbers. Leaves come in various sizes and shapes and with broad range of variegation.

Ipomoea: 'Morning Glory'. Annual. Blue, white, pink and red trumpet-shaped flowers. Climbs to at least 3 yards (metres) up almost anything.

Lathyrus odoratus: 'sweet pea'. Annual.

Scented climbers with pastel flowers in shades of pink, white, red, blue and lavender. Climb to 2 yards (metres) up wires, sticks or trellis.

Polygonum baldschuanicum: 'Russian vine or mile-a-minute plant'. Perennial. Will reach 20 yards (metres). Long sprays of white/pink flowers in summer. Climbs anything.

Thunbergia alata: 'Black-eyed Susan'. Annual. Golden or pale yellow flowers with brown centres. Climbs to 1–1.5 yards (metres). Requires a sheltered spot in full sun, with moist soil. Climbs unaided up a string, stick or trellis.

Tropaeolum majus: 'nasturtium'. Annual. Grows to 2 yards (metres), with orange yellow and deep red flowers. Training required. Full sun, dry soil.

FLOWERING PLANTS FOR SPRING

Azaleas: evergreen. Choose dwarf variety. Trumpet-shaped flowers in variety of colours. Lime-free soil. Shade.

Bellis perennis: white, pink and red daisies, double and single varieties. 4–6in (8–15cm).

Cheiranthus: 'wallflower'. Choose dwarf varieties. Bright colours, including red, yellow, orange and bronze. 6–12in (15–30cm).

Cineraria: large daisy-shaped flowers, usually in shades of blue, purple, pink and magenta. 8–12in (20–30cm).

Myosotis alpestris: 'forget-me-not'. Bright blue flowers, trailing habit. 6–12in (15–30cm).

Primula: 'primrose' and 'polyanthus'. Clear yellow, red, blue and purple flowers on

---

Old barrels and other containers are easily recycled to make planters. This one was found, appropriately enough, outside a pub and makes a bright contrast to the rather dull black paint of the building. The plants are a combination of bright red geraniums and green-yellow laurels. These colours always go well together, while orangey shades look better against darker green foliage.

PLANT LISTS

upright stems. 6–8in (15–20cm).

Rhododendron: evergreen. Choose dwarf evergreen variety. Trumpet-shaped flowers in a variety of colours. Lime-free soil. Shade.

Viola: 'pansy'. Range of colours. 4–6in (10–15cm).

FLOWERING PLANTS FOR AUTUMN

Chrysanthemum: choose 'pot chrysanthemums'. Daisy-style flowers in yellow, orange, red, rust and pink. 12–18in (30–45cm).

Cyclamen persicum: pink, white or red flowers on tall stems. Grey-green mottled leaves. 8–10in (20–25cm).

Erica carnea: 'winter-flowering heather'. White, pink, magenta shades. 6–10in (15–25cm).

Solanum capsicastrum: 'Christmas cherry'. Marble-sized orange fruits. Poisonous. Bushy green foliage. 12–18in (30–45cm).

FLOWERING PLANTS FOR WINTER

Camellia: flowers from mid-winter onwards, depending on cultivar. Evergreen. Plant in lime-free soil. Damp shade required.

Cyclamen persicum: pink, white and red flowers on tall, nodding stems. Grey-green mottled leaves. 8–10in (20–25cm).

Erica carnea: 'winter-flowering heather'. White, pink and magenta shades 6–10in (15–25cm).

Solanum capsicastrum: 'Christmas cherry'. Marble-sized orange fruits. Poisonous. Bushy

green foliage. 12–18in (30–45cm).

Viola: 'pansy'. Winter-flowering pansies are available in a broad range of colours, from yellow and apricot through to blue and purple. 4–6in (10–15cm).

SPRING BULBS

Chionodoxa luciliae: 'glory of the snow'. Bright blue flowers in mid/late spring. 6in (15cm).

Crocus: broad cup-shaped flowers in a range of colours, including blue, purple, yellow and white. They flower from early to late spring, depending on variety. Height ranges from 2½–4in (6–10cm).

Galanthus: 'snowdrop'. Small white bell-shaped flowers with narrow, spiky leaves, from early spring. 3½–4in (8–10cm).

Hyacinthus: scented spikes of flowers in pastel colours including pink, yellow, white and blue. Flower from mid-winter onwards, depending on the time they are planted. 6–10in (15–25cm).

Iris reticulata: dwarf iris, flowering from late winter. Colours include purple, blue and yellow. 6in (15cm).

Muscari armeniacum: 'grape hyacinth'. Purple-blue flowers on slim stems from mid-spring. 6–8in (15–20cm).

Narcissus: 'daffodil'. Bright yellow, pale yellow, cream, apricot and white trumpet flowers on tall stems. Choose dwarf or smaller varieties. Flowers from late winter to late

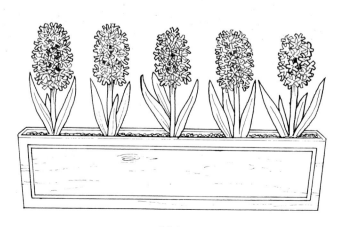

spring, depending on variety. Size ranges from 6–18in (15–45cm).

Scilla: brilliant blue bell-shaped flowers in early spring. Each plant produces several stems. 6in (15cm).

Tulipa: choose dwarf varieties for small troughs. Wide range of shapes, colours and sizes flowering from early to late spring. Height varies from 4–18in (10–45cm).

SUMMER BULBS

Summer windowboxes are best filled with annuals. There are a few summer bulbs suitable for troughs, but they are not highly recommended. You might consider:

Anemone 'de Caen': anemones in bright reds, purples, pinks and blues. Flowers in early to mid-summer. 12in (30cm).

Gladioli: choose smaller strains such as *Gladiolus byzantinus*, flowering in mid-summer.

24in (60cm) and taller.

Lilium: lilies. Look for short-growing hybrids. 24–36in (60–90cm).

AUTUMN BULBS

Colchicum: 'autumn crocus'. Large lilac-pink, mauve-pink, purple and white goblet-shaped flowers. Larger than the true crocus. 6–8in (15–20cm).

Crocus speciosus: true autumn-flowering crocus. Lilac, pink, white and violet colours. 4–5in (10–12cm).

Nerine bowdenii: round balls of pink flowers on tall stems. Flowers late autumn, early winter. 12–18in (30–45cm).

Sternbergia lutea: a crocus-like plant. It has golden yellow goblet-shaped flowers that open to 2in (5cm) in normal sunshine. Flowers from late summer to early autumn. 4in (10cm).

INDEX

INDEX

ACKNOWLEDGEMENTS

I should like to thank the following people for their assistance and advice:

Ian Adams
Sandra Ankarcrona
Armscote Manor Dried Flowers and
    Simon J. Lycett
Sydney Arrobus
Gyles and Michèle Brandreth
Mrs Joan Brown
Jenny Bunn
Mr and Mrs Chevalier
Creepers
Mary Douglas
Suchin Ee, Bexley, Kent
Mrs E Godfrey
Greenfingers Plant Displays of Forest Hill,
    London SE23

Catherine Horwood
Val Jackson
Geoffrey Kaye
Linda Morgan
Renaissance Casting – makers of lead
    containers
Muriel Riches
The Searle family
Stone Art
Mr B Weller, Bluebell Shop Arcades Ltd
Wisley Propagation Unit
And thank you to all the gardeners whose
wonderful windowboxes, hanging baskets
and containers are featured in these pages.